W9-BVJ-304

Seven Days
to
Faster Reading

Seven Days
to
Faster Reading

WILLIAM S. SCHAILL
President, The Reading Laboratory

HAWTHORN BOOKS, INC.   *Publishers*   NEW YORK

September, 1965

ACKNOWLEDGMENTS

"In the Beginning was the Word" is reprinted from *A History of Communications* by Maurice Fabre, volume 9 in *The New Illustrated Library of Science and Invention*, 1963, Hawthorn Books, Inc.

"Invaders Foiled" is reprinted from *Winston Churchill: A Memorial Edition*, a two-volume biography by Lewis Broad. Copyright © 1963 by Hawthorn Books, Inc.

"From Midway to Guadalcanal" is reprinted from *A Compact History of the U. S. Navy* (New and Revised Edition) by Fletcher Pratt and Hartley E. Howe. Copyright © 1962, 1957 by Hawthorn Books, Inc.

"The Shield of Achilles" is reprinted from *The Glory That was Greece* (New and Revised Edition) by J. C. Stobart and R. J. Hopper. Copyright © 1964 by Sidgewick & Jackson, Ltd.

"The Secret War of the OSS" is reprinted from *The Fighting Irishman: The Story of "Wild Bill" Donovan* by Maria Wilhelm. Copyright © 1964 by Hawthorn Books, Inc.

"Mohammed and Islam" is reprinted from *The Arabs: A Compact History* by Francesco Gabrieli. Copyright © 1963 by Hawthorn Books, Inc.

"The Earth from Space" is reprinted from *More Great True Adventures* selected by Lowell Thomas and Lowell Thomas, Jr. Copyright © 1963 by Hawthorn Books, Inc.

"Existentialism" is reprinted from *Life After Death* by Maurice and Louis Becqué, volume 28 in *The Twentieth Century Encyclopedia of Catholicism*. Copyright © 1960 by Hawthorn Books, Inc.

"When They First Shot the Tall American" is reprinted from *The Tall American: The Story of Gary Cooper* by Richard Gehman. Copyright © 1963 by Richard Gehman.

"Anglo-American Literature" is reprinted from *The Concise Encyclopedia of Modern World Literature* edited by Geoffrey Grigson. Copyright © 1963 by George Rainbird, Ltd.

"Mussolini's End" is reprinted from *Mussolini: A Study in Power* by Ivone Kirkpatrick. Copyright © 1964 by Ivone Kirkpatrick.

H-8085

FOREWORD

More and more people today find they must do more and more reading. Professional men, businessmen, and workers who want to get ahead faster in industry are learning that the road to advancement leads through masses of printed words. Men and women everywhere feel the need to absorb a flood of new information in order to understand thought currents moving through the world. They must read faster — and better.

With such a need apparent, the staff of *This Week Magazine* began a survey of the techniques which have developed the new methods of what may be called *Modern Reading*. We became convinced that these techniques produced dramatic results in faster reading time and were training people in a better, more intelligent way of reading.

Schools and colleges have discovered that courses in reading skills give enormous aid to students struggling under the heavier loads of today's scholastic programs. Young men and women trained in Modern Reading show distinct advantages over those who lack this kind of preparation.

A few years ago, as a service to the readers of our magazine, we decided to give them articles in the magazine which expressly dramatized the skills of Modern Reading. From the several authorities in the field we picked The Reading Laboratory of New York City and William S. Schaill, its president, as our consultants. The Reading Laboratory, organized in 1950, is one of the pioneers in developing the techniques of Modern Reading. From New York and other offices in Philadelphia, Princeton and San Francisco, this organization sends teams of experts into schools and colleges as well as into important business firms in this country and overseas to conduct executive courses in Advanced Modern Reading.

There was an immediate and favorable response to the articles in *This Week Magazine*. Now Mr. Schaill has decided to expand them into this book to serve both individual readers and teachers of reading. I am delighted to recommend Mr. Schaill's work. In keeping with the principles of reading faster, it will not take you long to learn from the book the method of Modern Reading. But, as Mr. Schaill points out, you must concentrate and drill yourself in the techniques until you practice them instinctively, and that takes longer. I believe the reward is with the fullness of effort.

In recent years millions of Americans have learned that it is not enough just to read *more*. Under today's information pressures you must read *faster* and *better*. It is the purpose of this book on Modern Reading to show you how.

William J. Nichols

Publisher and Editorial Director
This Week Magazine

New York
September 1965

Seven Days
to
Faster Reading

Contents

Part Three

PART ONE

Read Faster

Reading Rate Calculator Chart

To find your words-per-minute reading rate, take the total words in a selection you have just read and look for the number closest to this figure in the horizontal line at the top of the chart. Glance down this column till you reach the number opposite your reading time, as shown in the vertical column at the far left. This will be the approximate number of words you read per minute.

No. Words ➜	100	200	300	400	500	600	700	800	900	1000
No. Minutes ↓ 1	100	200	300	400	500	600	700	800	900	1000
1¼	80	160	240	320	400	480	560	640	720	800
1½	67	134	200	267	330	400	460	530	600	667
1¾	57	114	170	228	285	340	400	452	512	572
2	50	100	150	200	250	300	350	400	450	500
2¼	44	88	133	178	225	265	310	355	400	444
2½	40	80	120	160	200	240	280	320	360	400
2¾	36	72	109	146	180	218	255	290	325	364
3	33	66	100	133	165	200	232	265	300	333
3¼	31	62	92	123	155	185	215	245	276	308
3½	29	58	85	114	145	170	200	230	256	286
3¾	27	54	80	106	135	160	186	215	240	266
4	25	50	75	100	125	150	175	200	225	250
4¼	23	46	70	94	120	140	165	185	210	235
4½	22	44	67	89	110	133	155	177	200	222
4¾	21	42	63	85	105	127	147	169	190	210
5	20	40	60	80	100	120	140	160	180	200

Seven Days to
Faster Reading

YOU ARE ABOUT to have opened up to you a whole new world of reading pleasure. If reading has seemed difficult before, this book will show you how to make it almost effortless. I will tell you the skills by which rapid readers gain their speed, show you how to gain speed yourself. If you learn and practice the techniques and drills conscientiously your reading rate is bound to leap ahead. And as you read faster you will also read better. The purpose of this book is to tell you how.

The book is divided into three parts:

Part One tells you how to *read faster.*

Part Two tells you how to *read better.*

Part Three is made up of special selections from books covering a wide range of subjects. Here you can apply your new-found reading skills.

The book is dedicated to great reading and to your enjoyment of its wonders. This is a working manual, combining instruction with demonstrations of techniques and skills. The chapters are organized with planned repetition so that the method is drilled into you. It will have become an instinctive part of all your reading before you are through, and you will find your skill increasing from the very start. I believe that anyone who uses this book with serious application can double his reading speed.

Before going further, let's see what your normal reading speed is *now*. The selection that follows is from William Hickling Prescott's *Conquest of Mexico*, an American classic which chronicles the fall of Montezuma, King of the Aztec people, at the hands of Cortez and his conquistadors in 1519. The part I have chosen describes the fabulous "Halls of Montezuma" in what is today Mexico City.

To be fair, do not try to read faster than you would if you came across this section in the book. To time yourself you will need a clock or watch with a second hand. Pick a time in advance when you will start and note it down on the lines below.

_____ **MINUTES** _____ **SECONDS**

When the second hand reaches that point — *begin timing*.

MONTEZUMA encouraged a taste for architectural magnificence in his nobles and contributed his own share toward the embellishment of the city. Not content with the spacious residence of his father, Montezuma erected another on a yet more magnificent scale.

This pile of buildings spreads over an extent of ground so vast that, as one of the Conquerors assures us, its terraced roof might have afforded ample room for thirty knights to run their courses in a regular tourney. I have already noticed its interior decorations, its fanciful draperies, its roofs inlaid with cedar and other odoriferous woods, its numerous and spacious apartments which Cortez does not hesitate to declare superior to anything of the kind in Spain.

Adjoining the principal edifice was an armory, filled with the weapons and military dresses worn by the Aztecs, all kept in the most perfect order, ready for instant use. The emperor was himself very expert in the management of the Indian sword, and took great delight in witnessing athletic exercises and the mimic representation of war by his young nobility. Another building was used as a granary and others as warehouses for the different articles of food and apparel.

There was also an immense aviary, in which birds of splendid plumage were assembled from all parts of the empire. Here was the scarlet cardinal, the golden pheasant, the endless parrot tribe with their rainbow hues (the royal green predominant), and that miniature miracle of nature, the hummingbird, which delights to revel among the honeysuckle bowers of Mexico. Three hundred attendants had charge of the aviary and in the moulting season were careful to collect the beautiful plumage, which, with its many-colored tints, furnished the materials for the Aztec painter.

A separate building was reserved for the fierce birds of prey: the voracious vulture tribes and eagles of enormous size, whose home was in the snowy solitudes of the Andes. No less than five hundred turkeys, the cheapest meat in Mexico, were allowed for their daily consumption.

Adjoining this aviary was a menagerie of wild animals, gathered from the mountain forests and remote swamps. The collection was still further swelled by a great number of reptiles and serpents remarkable for their size and venomous qualities, among which the Spaniards beheld the rattlesnake, which they called "the fiery little animal with the castanets in his tail."

The serpents were confined in long cages lined with down or feathers, or in troughs of mud and water. The beasts and birds of prey were provided with apartments large enough to allow of their moving about and secured by a strong latticework, through which light and air were freely admitted.

Extensive gardens were spread out around the buildings. They were filled with fragrant shrubs and flowers and with various medicinal plants, the virtues of which were perfectly understood by the Aztecs. Fountains of pure water sparkled amidst this labyrinth of sweet-scented groves and shrubs. Light and fanciful pavilions, overlooking pools of limpid water, provided shelter in the heat of the Mexican summer.

But the most luxurious residence of the Aztec monarch was the royal hill of Chapultepec, consecrated by the ashes of his ancestors. It stood west of the capital, surrounded by the waters of the Tezcuco River. On its lofty crest of red-purple rock there now stands the magnificent, though desolate, castle, erected by the young viceroy Galvez, at the close of the seventeenth century. The view from its windows is one of the finest in Mexico, and Montezuma's gardens stretch for miles around the base of the hill. Even today they are still shaded by gigantic cypresses, more than fifty feet in circumference, which were centuries old at the time of Cortez.

Stop Timing Finish time ___6___ **MINUTES** ___45___ **SECONDS**

To find out your reading score, use the chart on page 8. The selection contains about 630 words. Or you can find your score this way:

Multiply 630 by 60 and you get 37800.

Figure the number of seconds it took you to read the selection. Suppose it was 145 seconds. Divide 37800 by 145. The answer is the reading score — 260 words per minute.

Using the number of seconds you actually took in reading the selection, figure your score and write it on the line at the right below. This is your first timing test and represents the speed at which you normally read at present.

ORIGINAL TIMING SCORE _____ **WPM**

WHATEVER YOUR SPEED, now put away your watch and concentrate on the two sets of points we are going to cover in the rest of this chapter. These consist, first, of the three basic concepts of the method by which you read faster and better and, second, the seven steps by which you will achieve reading speed.

The Three Basic Concepts

1. The Concept of Eye Movement. Everyone reads — *but*, with most people it is a haphazard process. You learned to read in the first grade and you read more and more as you grew older. But did you ever stop to think that in all probability no one ever taught you *how* to read? I mean that no one explained the mechanics or physiology of reading and told you how to make these natural processes work for you to develop speed and quicker comprehension.

For example, when you pick up a letter, a newspaper, a magazine or a book your eyes *seem* to move smoothly over the lines of type from left to right. But the truth is, they move in a series of jerks. Your eyes stop — "fixate," the experts call it — and register a word or two. Then they jerk to the right and repeat the process until you have read the entire line. You read only during the stops or fixations.

To test this, use the card which is inserted in this copy of your book. Read the instructions on the card and ask someone to check your eye movements by looking through the peephole. Try the same experiment on your partner. Focus on one of his eyes through the peephole and watch it jump from left to right as he reads the lines of type. There are ten words in the top line on the card. If his eye jerks ten times he is a word-by-word reader. More about that later.

2. The Concept of the Eye-Mind Relationship. We read with the eyes, of course. But the eyes are only a camera which photographs images for the mind to translate into ideas. It is the mind which preserves what you read — not the eyes. But since the mind can receive its images only through the eyes, the eyes must be trained to record these word images swiftly and surely.

3. The Concept of Reading Purpose. From now on you will approach everything you read *with a purpose*. You will undertake many kinds of reading for many purposes. Both comprehension and retention are sharpened when your purpose is fixed in advance. You will not waste time in letting your eyes wander vaguely down the page. You will put system and efficiency into your reading.

This kind of selectivity is as much one of the skills of Modern Reading as increasing speed. Remember, you don't have to read every word on every piece of paper that comes across your desk. The efficient way is to make a quick estimate of its nature and its value to you. Then decide if and how you will read it. This can save many minutes out of your working day.

You apply this same evaluation to everything you read, whether it is for information only, for entertainment or for the sheer pleasure of self-enrichment through a finely written novel or a biography. You establish in advance *the purpose* for which you are reading.

People who have not yet learned the total conception of Modern Reading often ask two questions: "If I learn to read rapidly, won't I miss a great deal — particularly the beauty of imaginative writing?" And, "Won't I overlook important points if I go through articles so fast?"

Experience shows that the rapid reader remembers far more — not less — of what he reads, because he has learned to be an efficient reader. Understanding is increased because he knows *why* he reads and because he concentrates. As to missing beauty, Modern Reading calls for changes of speed with different kinds of reading material. The trained reader slows down when he wants to savor the beauty of poetry, of drama, of fine passages in a biography or novel. He paces himself to what he is reading.

So now you have the three basic concepts of Modern Reading:

1. A thorough grasp of the *eye-movement mechanics* which will govern many of the techniques in faster reading I shall show you later.

2. An understanding of the *eye-mind relationship* which conditions the comprehension and retention of what you read.

3. An awareness of your *reading purpose before* you begin to read. This causes you to read different kinds of material at different speeds and reduces the over-all time you spend on reading. Remember the concepts and you will see just how the skills of Modern Reading grow out of them.

Now WE ARE READY to consider the skills and techniques by which you increase actual reading speed. Each of these is fully developed in the seven chapters that follow, but I think a quick summary will help you to see this entire method in perspective.

Seven Days to Faster Reading

1. You pre-read first. Before you begin to read anything you establish your purpose and then give a quick, searching scrutiny. If it is a magazine article, for example, you

- *a.* Read the title and explanatory subheads.
- *b.* Note the author's name.
- *c.* Look at illustrations and read captions.
- *d.* Read any bold-face or italic material, lettered or numbered points, any boxes or graphs.

The next chapter explains this process as it applies to various kinds of reading. The point I want to make here is that by pre-reading you decide how much of the article it will be useful for you to read. Sometimes pre-reading will give you all you need to know of an article, with a consequent saving of time.

As a Modern Reader you do not read everything you come across. You are selective. You ask your *purpose* before plunging ahead and discovering ten or fifteen minutes later that you are wasting your time. One of the means of getting through the mass of reading material that presents itself to all of us — — *Businessmen, please note* — is *not reading* unless you are sure you must. But bear in mind that sheer enjoyment of good writing is one of the best purposes of all.

2. You read in phrases. The speed at which you read a line of type depends directly on the number of stops, or fixations, your eyes make. In a line of twelve words, if your eyes take in only a single word each time they stop they must make twelve fixations. (And some poor readers take in only *part* of a word at each fixation!) If you widen your recognition span to take in two words, the fixations are cut in half — to six. If your eyes can take in three words at each stop, the fixations are reduced to four! It is obvious that this is one of the first concerns of rapid reading. The more your eyes absorb in each fixation, the more you cut reading time. I'll explain the drills to accomplish this in Chapter Two.

3. You concentrate when you read. The greatest impediment to efficient and retentive reading is inattention. Your mind must be fully engaged. You must not let your thoughts wander while your eyes follow the lines of type. Unless you concentrate the eyes do not transmit clear images to the mind.

Lack of attention is reflected in what we call "regressions."

The unsure reader casts his eyes back a word or two, or a line or two, because he is afraid he has missed something. With untrained readers this fault is habitual, and it is a killer to rapid reading because it slows the pace with interruptions. Unless a reader concentrates and keeps his mind engaged, these regressions will continue to plague him, and he will never become an efficient, rapid reader.

4. You practice the drills of rapid reading. To attain speed you must constantly stretch your performance beyond what is a comfortable pace. To accomplish this goal you must widen your span of recognition through techniques explained in Chapter Four. You must also quicken the *perception rate* at which the mind recognizes and accepts word images from the eyes. You will learn flash techniques to overcome "lazy vision." You will be taught to focus your eyes just above a line of type rather than directly on it, a technique which tends to make phrases stand out. These drills are to rapid reading what finger exercises are to a piano student. They provide the practice which is essential to acquire smooth performance.

5. You master skipping and skimming. These are skills which all Modern Readers use to get through material quickly. But there is a pattern to both. They are not haphazard movements of your eyes over a page of type. The technique is in learning how to skip and skim with confidence that you are missing nothing important. The correct methods are described in Chapter Five.

6. You build your vocabulary. Rapid, efficient reading depends above all else on a wide vocabulary. You cannot read rapidly unless your mind recognizes instantly the images of words and phrases which your eyes transmit. If your vocabulary is limited you must work to build it.

Most people have a vocabulary which can be divided into three categories: *Active* (words they use regularly in speech); *Reserve* (words they know but do not use in conversation, though they may in writing); and *Passive* (words they recognize as images when they come across them but are never quite aware of what they mean and so never use them). If this is a fair estimate of your own vocabulary — and it probably is — your target is not only to acquire new words but to move words from your *reserve* and *passive* categories into your *active* vocabulary. Remember, you are never quite sure of a word until you speak it and use it in conversation.

7. You learn to pick your reading speed. As I stated earlier in this Introduction, you will learn to adjust your speed to the kind of reading you are doing, no matter how rapidly you *can* read. You don't drive your car at the same speed all the time. You are guided by the condition of the road, of traffic and the nature of your errand. In the same way, you don't try to race through Shakespeare or an article on astrophysics. You change speeds and gear your pace to what you are reading.

Now THAT YOU have been shown *Seven Days to Faster Reading*, let me sum up the objectives you are going to reach by using this book. The chances are that you are not now a really efficient reader, acutely conscious of how to read with a purpose. You let your mind wander as you look at a page and so you do not comprehend or retain at your full potential. The target is to adjust all your senses to complete involvement in the reading process. You must be alert, absorbed, in a mood to anticipate the author's next words. Your attention must be fully engaged.

To prove to yourself what this can do for you, I want you to take another timing test now. But this time you are to stretch yourself, concentrate, read with all your senses alert and your mind fully engaged from start to finish. Without losing comprehension, read as fast as you can. This selection is a continuation of the Montezuma story, so the style and reading level are the same as for the first test. Take out your watch or look at the clock and get set to go.

_____15_____ **MINUTES** _____30_____ **SECONDS**

Start Timing

THE domestic establishment of Montezuma was on the same scale of barbaric splendor as everything else about him. He could boast as many wives as were found in the harem of an Eastern sultan. These were lodged in apartments, provided with every accommodation for personal comfort and cleanliness. They passed their hours in weaving and embroidery and especially in the graceful featherwork, for which materials were furnished by the royal aviaries.

They conducted themselves with strict decorum, under the supervision of aged females, who acted in the capacity of duennas. The palace was supplied with numerous baths, and Montezuma himself set the example of frequent ablutions. He bathed at least once and changed his dress four times every day. He never put on the same dress for a second time but gave it away to his attendants. Not even his contemporary — Elizabeth I — could afford such costly habits.

His meals the emperor took alone. The well-matted floor of a large saloon was covered with hundreds of dishes, kept hot over the flame. The royal bill of fare included game from the distant forests and fish which, the day before, had been swimming in the Gulf of Mexico.

The meats were served by the attendant nobles and maidens selected for their personal grace and beauty. A screen of richly gilt and carved wood was drawn around the emperor so as to conceal him from vulgar eyes while he ate. He was seated on a cushion, and his dinner was served on a low table covered with a delicate cotton cloth. The dishes were of the finest ware of Cholula, and the entire table service was never allowed to appear a second time but was given away to the attendants. The dining room was lighted by torches made of a resinous wood, which sent forth a sweet odor as they burned.

The emperor never took any other beverage than the *chocolatl*, a drink of chocolate flavored with vanilla and other spices and reduced to a froth of the consistency of honey, which gradually dissolved in the mouth. This beverage was served in golden goblets, with spoons of the same metal or of finely wrought tortoise shell.

The dessert of the Aztec emperor was an assortment of fruits gathered fresh from the luscious trees of the tropics, plucked from green groves and transmitted by means of courier to the capital. After the royal appetite was appeased, water was handed to him by female attendants in a silver basin; pipes were brought, made of a varnished and richly gilt wood, from which Montezuma inhaled the fumes of an intoxicating weed, "called *tobacco*," mingled with liquid amber. While smoking, he enjoyed the exhibitions of his mountebanks and jugglers, of whom a regular corps was attached to the palace. No people, not even those of China or Hindustan, surpassed the Aztecs in feats of agility.

When he had sufficiently refreshed his spirits with these various diversions, the emperor composed himself to sleep, for in his siesta he was as regular as any Spaniard. On awakening, he gave audience to ambassadors from foreign states, or his own tributary cities, or to such chiefs as had suits to prefer to him.

They were introduced by the young nobles in attendance, and, whatever might be their rank, unless of the blood royal, they were obliged to submit to the humiliation of shrouding their rich dresses with the coarse mantle of sackcloth and entering barefooted, with downcast eyes, into the presence.

The emperor addressed brief remarks to the suitors, and the parties retired with the same reverential obeisance, taking care to keep their faces turned toward the monarch. Well might Cortez exclaim that no court, whether of the Grand Seigneur or any other infidel, ever displayed so pompous and elaborate a ceremonial!

The maintenance of this court of several thousands of individuals involved heavy expenditures and required complicated accounts. But everything in Montezuma's household was conducted with perfect order; all the various receipts and disbursements were set down in the picture writing of the country. The arithmetical characters were even more refined than the ones used for letters.

Such was the picture of Montezuma's domestic establishment and way of living, as Cortez and his followers saw it.

Stop Timing Finish time: |—4— **MINUTES** —30— **SECONDS**

This selection is approximately 730 words. My guess is that you raced through it at a far faster rate than you scored on the first. This time you read with your senses alert. You were concentrated on the words. Your mind was fully engaged. Now use the chart or the simple mathematical formula I gave you to figure your reading speed and see how much better you did this time. Write in your score.

SECOND TIMING SCORE _162_ **WPM**

This is Modern Reading, and it can revolutionize your life. It works — if *you* work. When you have mastered the method in this book you will find that your reading speed is vastly increased — perhaps even doubled. And you will have opened up a source of rich enjoyment.

CHAPTER ONE

First Day: Pre-reading

P<small>RE-READING</small> applies entirely to nonfiction. It is not part of rapid reading as such, though it must be done quickly or its value as a timesaver is lost. It means simply that instead of beginning to read blindly you give a fast preliminary survey to every article, report, long business letter or nonfiction book to see what it is about and estimate its usefulness *to you*. If it has value, you go back and read the whole thing. But when a reader becomes skilled in this technique, pre-reading will often supply the gist of an entire article.

The Technique of Pre-reading

1. Magazine articles. Read the title first, with any subtitles which accompany it. This will give you a general idea of the subject. Note the author's name and, if it is not familiar, look for explanatory facts about him on the page. These will provide a gauge of the article's authority. Examine charts, graphs, boldface material and numbered points. Look at photographs and read their captions.

Next, read the first few paragraphs thoroughly, since these will contain the writer's approach to his subject. Once his theme is stated, read only first sentences of succeeding paragraphs. If the article is well organized, these should be *topic sentences*, each introducing the subject of the paragraph. Toward the end of the article, when the author begins to give his conclusions, start reading thoroughly again.

In the briefest possible time you have now pre-read an article with one or more of these results:

a. You have the gist of the article and do not need to read it thoroughly — an efficient saving of time.

b. You know that it has a great deal of important new information and will repay thorough reading.

c. Your pre-reading has provided double insurance of retention since when you read thoroughly you will go over the important facts again. Your mind also has a logical framework on which to hang other facts.

2. Business reports. These can put a heavy load on any businessman's day, and the technique of handling them is quite similar to pre-reading magazine articles. Your first look is to determine whether a particular report is about a phase of the business that concerns *you*. If it isn't, you may seem justified in filing it unread or tossing it into your wastebasket. But better page through it first. Read the first two or three paragraphs, turn the pages rapidly and stop for tables of figures or statistics to make sure they can safely be skipped. Look for topic headings and skim the conclusion. (See Chapter Five for skimming technique.) It may be that some distant division manager has made a recommendation which directly affects your own activity.

3. Business letters. A quick three-step treatment helps get through a pile of these. A glance at the letterhead and then at the signature yields an immediate estimate of the letter's probable importance to you. Most letters come directly to the point, as any good letter should. But sometimes introductory paragraphs are evasive or unconsciously windy. In such cases, jump almost two-thirds of the way through the letter, where the central point is apt to be hidden.

4. Research. Pre-reading is invaluable for anyone collecting material to be used in an article, a paper, a speech or a book. When he begins his research in a library, the writer is simply noting down items which seem to touch on his subject. Then, instead of spending hours reading through this mass of material, pre-reading quickly informs him whether a particular title is worth reading further. Instead of aimlessly skimming, the efficient researcher streamlines his task by pre-reading.

5. Books. When you are not sure that you want to spend the time reading a book of nonfiction, pre-reading supplies the basis of decision. The author and title will have attracted you, of course, but titles are sometimes misleading, designed to catch the eye rather than provide a key to the subject. A subtitle may help to explain it, but in most cases a reading of the inside jacket flaps provides both a quick summary of the book and a brief biography of the author.

If your interest is caught, look at the table of contents. The author's introduction is also useful, since here he usually states his purpose in writing the book. Many books of nonfiction are as enthralling as anything the novelist contrives, and there is no hesitation on the reader's part in plunging in. But a little pre-reading will still serve to put you in the author's mood and make reading more enjoyable. And if it is a biography or history, you need not feel you are cheating if you read the last chapter for the author's summing up. Your enjoyment and understanding of the whole book will be enhanced if you have a good idea of the author's conclusions.

5a. Chapters of books. When you are in doubt about the value of reading a book of nonfiction you can apply the pre-reading technique to the early chapters. My own advice is to pre-read the first two or three, then turn to the last two chapters in which the author will recapitulate and summarize. This is a particularly valuable skill for college students to acquire — the sooner the better. Freshmen often feel a sense of bewilderment at the size of their reading assignments and many fail because they never learn how to adjust themselves to the load. The answer is so simple. Pre-reading an entire textbook provides an over-all view of what the course is about. Then the student has a comfortable idea of where he is going. He knows what to expect and is prepared for it. This is true not only of textbooks but of the massive supplementary reading required by colleges. Students can extend pre-reading here to a quick look in an encyclopedia to get an estimate of an author, his place in literature and history.

6. Newspapers. Pre-reading does not apply to news stories. Indeed, newspapers are designed for a special type of pre-reading. The headline and subheads tell what the story is about. The most important facts are in the first few sentences — the "lead." For example:

> "*Keeping guards and customers at bay with submachine guns, two masked men held up the Tenth National Bank shortly after noon today and escaped with loot estimated at $30,000.*"

So the lead of a news story might read. The account will continue to supply supplementary facts, but they will become less and less important. They will be details that are pertinent and interesting but can be safely skipped now that you have the main outline of the story.

This style of organization does not apply to other parts of the newspaper. Columnists, special stories, editorials, book and dramatic reviews may be pre-read if you wish, though the newspaper is a matter of such immediate interest that pre-reading should be of the quickest sort, a kind of in and out technique which you will develop at your own pace.

Begin to Practice Pre-reading Now

Pre-reading is the first of the seven steps to faster reading. To make it work for you, the technique must become a habit. You must remember to practice it with every piece of non-fiction you come across. You have set out to become a better and a faster reader. You are going to do it yourself, without the discipline which regular classroom sessions provide. To succeed, you must consciously adopt the techniques of Modern Reading with everything you read. Don't concentrate on them only in the work periods you set yourself when you are using this book. Use them constantly. In that way you acquire the habit.

It is important to remember that pre-reading is a quick once-over. Do not allow yourself to make it a leisurely survey from which you suddenly burst into a flurry of rapid reading. That's not what pre-reading is for. Its first purpose is saving time. This goal will be lost unless you press yourself to reach conclusions swiftly.

CHAPTER TWO

Second Day:
Phrase Reading

THE BASIC SKILL of rapid reading is learning to *read in phrases.* This simply means taking wider "visual bites" as your eyes move across a line of type. As I explained in the Introduction, your eyes read words in a series of stops, or "fixations," jerking to the right after each stop to take in the next portion of the line. You read only when your eyes are stopped. The more words you can take in at each bite, the fewer stops will be necessary on each line and the faster you will read. By widening what is called your "span of recognition" you automatically increase your reading speed.

To test your present *span of recognition* try focusing your eyes on the sixth word in the next line. Although you will be consciously fixed on a single word, your *span of recognition* should let you read the word to the left and the word to the right — perhaps a bit more. As you practice stretching your *side-vision* the span of recognition will widen, and you will absorb more words with each fixation.

If you were reading a list of unrelated words you would have to read word by word. But in normal reading the words are held together by the broader meaning of phrases and sentences. Sentences are made up of *units of meaning.* The eyes and mind can be trained to absorb these *units of meaning* far more readily if you read in phrases rather than at the plodding rate of one word at a time.

Changing from reading word by word to phrase reading will not only increase your reading speed. It will also quicken your comprehension. The word-by-word reader is getting his information too slowly to occupy his mind. The slow reader can *think* much faster than he can *read*. His mind is not fully engaged by the ideas on the page because they enter too slowly. His thoughts wander. Other ideas come in. Before long, the reader is not concentrating on the meaning of what his eyes see because he is unable to keep his mind fully involved.

The phrase reader will not encounter this problem of lagging attention. He receives ideas from the printed page rapidly enough to keep his mind engaged with the matter in hand. This is because he is reading in the same way he thinks — by a close approximation of whole ideas. Instead of gradually building up a thought pattern word by word, he grasps it whole — just as it was in the author's mind. Because he is in more immediate contact with the author, comprehension is inevitably improved, and with it retention of the facts and ideas he has read. His mind has received the images clearly — and they stick.

The Three Kinds of Readers

To understand more clearly how phrase reading improves skill, let's find out what kind of reader you are *now*. There are three types, and it is a simple matter to test yourself.

First, the *motor reader*. He forms words with his lips, just as though he were reading aloud, and so he can grasp only one word at a time. You could still be a motor reader, even though your lips do not move. Give yourself this test: Put your fingers on your throat. Now go on reading. If you feel any movement in your larynx now (except from the pulse there), you are still a motor reader, grasping only one word at a time. This means that you can read silently only as fast as you can read aloud.

Second, the *auditory reader:* Though his lips and larynx do not move, he hears every word in his "mind's ear." You can test yourself on this, too. Open a novel, if you have one handy, though any book will do. Fix your eyes on a page but before you start reading say aloud some such nonsense phrase as "Mary had a little lamb." Repeat it several times and then start reading, still saying aloud "Mary had a little lamb" as you try to read. If you are unable to comprehend what you are reading — if the words are just a meaningless jumble — then you are definitely an auditory reader.

Even though you understood fully what you were reading in spite of the nonsense you were repeating, you could still be an auditory reader. Read the next few paragraphs in the book on which you have just tested yourself. Now stop and think back. Were you conscious that you were reading words? Did you hear them in your head? Then I am afraid you are still an auditory reader.

The auditory reader can read much faster than the motor reader, but he is still handicapped in reaching high speed, because he is held back by the necessity of "hearing" words in his head.

Third, the *sight reader:* With him, the eye-mind relationship I described in the Introduction is fully adjusted. His eyes photograph words which are translated by the mind instantly into ideas without the aid of either the vocal or auditory senses. Obviously he has a head start toward becoming a rapid reader as quickly as he is trained in the techniques which will make him aware of how to use his talent.

Practice in Phrase Reading

One of the quickest ways to progress from being a motor or an auditory reader to the goal of sight reading is to practice phrase reading. Here are three exercises that will drill you, and you should come back to them periodically for review.

Exercise 1: Use the eye-swing chart below. Glance briefly at each solid bar, making fast swings from line to line as you go through the motions of reading.

The spacing in the three lines below provides the same sort of eye-swing practice. Read with a conscious swing of the eyes; it will accustom you to your new reading technique.

> This is   one of   the best   means of
> training your eyes   to accustom themselves
> to the rhythm   of big visual bites   as you read.

Exercise 2: Use the phrase-reading part of the Pacing Card inserted in this book to read rapidly down the columns below. Fit the cut-out upper left-hand corner of the card so the phrases appear just to the left. Now draw the card evenly down each of the columns, making just one fixation on the first and second and no more than two fixations on the third column. The purpose of the exercise is not only to give you phrase-reading practice but to quicken the time you spend on each fixation. This is another way to speed up your reading.

The bigger	In phrase reading	The sight reader understands
the bite	you get much more	what he reads far better
of a line	of the meaning	than the motor or auditory
of type	at a single gulp	reader because his mind
you train	and so it is	receives more of the sense
yourself	easier to grasp	each time the eyes fixate
to take,	the full sense	and is therefore able
the faster	of what you read	to translate the phrases
you read.	in less time.	into the author's ideas.

Exercise 3: To become an efficient phrase reader you need to make yourself conscious of the *units of meaning* in sentences. One of the simplest ways to do this is to take your newspaper and circle these units with a pencil. Do not expect them all to be just two or three words long. Some will contain more than you are able to take in with a single fixation. What you are now training yourself to do to stretch your skill by forcing your mind to anticipate words or parts of words that lie ahead.

This is where a widened span of recognition helps. For example, in reading you come to the phrase, "words hard to understand." By the time you have seen "un-" or at most "under-" you know that "understand" will be the word from the sense of what has gone before and you skip on to the next unit. Circling phrases for a while will drill you to anticipate phrase endings and therefore increase reading speed.

When circling seems clumsy you can accomplish the same purpose by marking off / units of meaning / like this. / The important thing / is to practice / this kind of drill / till it becomes / second nature. /

After you have circled units of meaning or marked them off by diagonal lines, go back and read over the paragraphs several times. Stretch yourself to read as rapidly as you can, being conscious of jumping from phrase to phrase. Practice this exercise 15 minutes each day.

At first this is a conscious process, and its goal is to make you anticipate as your eyes fixate on a phrase. The ease with which you do this depends on the sort of material you have selected to read. If the subject is unfamiliar and the words difficult, your "bites" will be smaller than if you were reading, say, a mystery novel. But with practice the span of recognition gradually widens for all kinds of material. An improved reading rate comes from a combination of widened recognition and sharpened alertness, plus the skill of anticipating parts of a word or even whole words that lie ahead.

This makes as good an answer as I know to the question, "But if I learn to read twice as fast as I am reading now, doesn't it mean that I won't take in what I read?" You will take in far more, because you are drilling yourself to do just that. You cannot become a *faster* reader without becoming at the same time a *more efficient* reader. Faster reading and greater comprehension are twin goals and twin rewards of acquiring Modern Reading skill.

CHAPTER THREE

Third Day: Concentration

THE EFFECTIVENESS of every part of the Modern Reading technique is dependent on the ability to submerge yourself completely in the reading process. *Concentration* is the secret. You cannot read at your fastest speed and still get all the meaning unless you *concentrate*.

Ask yourself these three questions:

1. *"Do I really concentrate now when I read?"*

2. *"Am I so thoroughly engrossed that exterior noises will not make me look up?"*

3. *"Can I control my mind with such discipline that it stays fixed on what I read and will not be disturbed by remembering a phone call I should make, a bill that needs paying?"*

If such thoughts creep in, your mind is not thoroughly engaged when you read. You have not learned to concentrate.

This is a discipline you must train yourself to follow at a moment's notice. If your attention is caught by a newspaper headline, and you pick up the paper, read the story with concentration. Otherwise you might just as well leave it unread.

The headline impressed you because it was big and black. You'll remember that. But you will remember very little of the news story unless for the few minutes it takes you to read it your whole attention is involved.

You can test this in a very simple way. Most people have the habit of reading a newspaper in the morning, either at home or on the way to work. For the next few days make sure the newspaper is saved or bring it home with you. Reread the stories you read in the morning. Ask yourself honestly if you recall the details. If someone had brought up one of the stories during the day, would your recollection have been so clear that you could talk about the situation intelligently?

These are fair questions, and I hope you can answer "Yes" with a clear conscience. But as a man who has given retention tests to a good many thousands of Modern Reading students, I will tell you that until you train yourself to concentrate you do not remember nearly as much as you thought you did if leading questions are asked. Most people, men and women, read aimlessly. Their minds are only partially engaged. Unless you involve your mind fully you will never become an efficient rapid reader.

Concentration is something of a trick — to be learned like all the techniques of Modern Reading. At home or in the office — you will do most of your reading in those two places — you can ease the process by creating the right environment. Make sure your light is good — sunlight or a 100-watt lamp, but avoid glare by having at least one other light source in the room. Pick a chair that is comfortable but not too relaxing. That old cliché of "curling up with a good book" is bad advice for Modern Readers. With a little experience, you will find you are far more comfortable if you sit upright — and a great deal more alert. The most satisfactory position for reading is the one the orthopedists recommend: a firm, straight chair with your lower back firmly pressed against the back of the chair.

Lean slightly forward, but keep upright. You can sit this way for long periods without feeling fatigued.

It is useful, of course, whether you are at home or in the office, to shut out distracting noises by closing the door. This helps you to relax from tensions and fix your mind on what you are about to read. If you are at home the closed door may shut out the insistent music and voices of television or radio from another part of the house. Hold the book, magazine or newspaper in your hands if you wish. I think the more comfortable position is to rest it on a desk or table. But make sure it is at a correct angle and at the proper distance from your eyes so that you see the type without strain.

After exterior noise, the greatest enemy of concentration is worry or emotional problems. There is no general cure for these, but I can suggest a therapy that sometimes works. If you have something on your mind, take positive action before you start reading. Is there an important phone call you must make at ten o'clock and now it is only eight? Then write yourself a note: "Call So-and-So at ten." If there is nothing you can do until tomorrow, at least you can relieve tension by trying to plan definite action and promising yourself that you will solve the problem next morning. This may seem like something of a subterfuge but it will often calm anxieties so you can concentrate.

Reading With a Purpose

With distractions out of the way, you are ready to practice the technique of concentrating. And it *is* a technique. You may think now that it comes naturally but you should understand clearly the processes by which your mind becomes engaged. *Reading with a purpose* is the most important, and let's see how this works with a few examples:

a. You pick up your newspaper. A crisis has developed

somewhere in the world. Information is your purpose. You are eager for details. You absorb yourself to learn what this new crisis may mean.

b. There was a big pro football game yesterday. You know how it came out but you want to learn what the experts thought. You're not so much seeking information as a Monday morning quarterback's estimate of the game. But you concentrate on the expert's rundown because you want to talk with friends about it later.

c. You have a book — a biography. It is a big best-seller, and you think you will enjoy reading it. You will be reading purely for enjoyment and self-enrichment. To be sure, you will gain information and the interpretation of events and character. But the promise of the book is that it will plunge you into the sheer enjoyment of a reading experience. That is your goal for the evening, and you let it enfold you completely.

Just how do you involve yourself in these several reading experiences? You do not let yourself become a passive reader. You adopt a questioning attitude. Is the correspondent reporting objectively on the crisis situation about which he writes? Is the football expert biased or does he give a fair enough estimate on the game? Is the biographer trying to persuade you to a particular point of view about his subject? You read with this kind of question in your mind.

It becomes a sort of game which enormously increases your enjoyment of reading. You already know the purpose with which you read the article or book. But what was the author's purpose? Was he honest in what he told you? Was he trying to mislead you to establish a certain point of view? Has an argument been built up which you can demolish because of your knowledge of the facts?

These are questions which will crowd your mind when you

are "concentrated." They will not even occur if you are not fully involved, and you will miss half the pleasure of reading. When concentration is complete it will shut out everything else. You will begin to anticipate what the author is going to say next. You will almost feel that he is in the room with you and that you are engaged in a personal argument. When you reach such an attitude your mind is fully engaged.

Concentrating is a skill you can practice every day — at home or when you are reading in your office. It won't be easy at first, and there are no exercises that can help you. Mastering the technique is sheer will power at work, for you must discipline yourself. What is required is that you learn to detach your mind from, first, the distractions of the exterior world and, second, the inner anxieties of your emotions so that it becomes absorbed in a third reality — what lies on the printed page before you.

You will know you have succeeded when you can study a business report undisturbed by spike-heel shoes clattering up and down the corridor outside your office. When a book completely absorbs you at home with children's voices outside your open window and a record player blaring across the street, then you have acquired the trick of concentration. And you have taken a giant step toward faster — and better — reading.

Fourth Day: Speed Drills

IT IS TIME NOW to introduce you to the drills which will put speed into your reading. You have learned about phrase reading and why it automatically increases your speed. I have told you that you cannot reach speed and comprehension unless you give full concentration while you read.

Just how fast should you be able to read? What about these claims of people who read 5,000 and 10,000 words a minute? All I can say is that I do not know any such geniuses, though they may exist. I don't know anyone personally who breaks the four-minute mile, though it has been done by a number of outstanding runners.

Unless you have exceptional ability to begin with, I should say your target would be 600 to 800 words a minute. If you can consistently read 800 words a minute on average narrative material, that's 48,000 words an hour, which means that you could read a book of 100,000 words — a good-sized novel or biography — in an evening.

Now let's concentrate on the drills which will increase your speed. These have principally to do with learning to move through material with the phrase-reading technique I have explained, stretching your speed constantly beyond the rate at which you easily read.

Columnar Reading

I often say that your newspaper is one of the best tools for the practice of Modern Reading. This is what I mean: Because of its narrow columns you can move down the lines of a newspaper easily and with few fixations per line. To stretch yourself, draw a line down the middle of any newspaper column. Focus on the line and try to stretch your span of recognition as far as you can on both sides to take in the words as your eyes slide rapidly down the center of the column. You won't be able to do this successfully at first. But practice the drill. As you work you will find you anticipate words and meanings, as I explained in Chapter Two. Focusing on the center line and going down the column, you will be able to comprehend more and more until you are reading almost everything in the column.

For practice, try the technique with columns of phrases. The drill with the columns below is exactly the same as that you were shown in Chapter Two, with the exception of the fact that these phrases are unrelated to each other. Use the cut-out portion of your Pacing Card.

out of town	psychological moment	for one reason or another
flying high	local representative	Associated Press dispatch
carpet tack	crude-oil production	synthetic textile fabrics
many reasons	of all requirements	a new brand of cigarettes
best results	accidents do happen	Republic of South Africa
good weather	profit-sharing plans	I shall be most grateful
market value	Republican candidate	civil-service examination
heavy smoker	at an annual rate of	the verdict was "guilty"
the white cat	increasing broadness	political representative
five-day week	government operation	at the regular list price

Pace Your Practice Reading

Now I want you to begin stretching your reading speed. Take the Pacing Card which came with this book (any card will do here) and, using your newspaper, place the card so that it is just above any column. Now, as you did in columnar reading, focus your eyes on the middle of the column. Draw the card down in an even motion — faster than you can comfortably read — and try to get every fact in the story. Do not go back during this exercise or let your eyes regress. If you think you missed something, don't worry about it. Keep going. Bring the card to the end of the column and now test yourself by asking questions. Try to restate the principal facts, the main ideas. Then spend as much time as you want going back through the column to find how much you missed.

This kind of drill is going to concern you for quite some time, if you are to become a really rapid reader. You are to read newspapers, magazines, books — using the card or a piece of paper to pace yourself. You must draw it down evenly over the lines of type, catch the meaning in a line as the card uncovers it and then move your eyes down to the next. You must draw the card down in even rhythm. But you will soon find that you are speeding the rhythm with practice. This is quite an exciting discovery. Time yourself each day on different sorts of material — using the mathematical formula in the Introduction or the chart to calculate your reading time per minute — and see how your speed grows.

Flash Reading

One technique of Modern Reading is to increase the speed of your recognition of *word images* and *numbers*. In classrooms students receive extensive practice with what is called a "phrase-flasher". This is an individual aid which exposes phrases or digits for a predetermined length of time and then wipes them out something like a flashing sign. The purpose of this kind of training is to quicken perception so that your eyes fixate instantly on several words or numbers at one time. With phrases, your mind receives word images so rapidly that ideas build one from another and there is no lag during which thoughts can wander.

You can approximate this drill by using the Pacing Card. Ask someone to make you two or three columnar lists. Start with short words and work up to phrases about fourteen letters in length. The drill is simply to place the card above the first phrase, draw it down and back as quickly as you can. In the brief exposure you read the phrase. Then bring the card down to the top of the next phrase and repeat the process.

Digit drill is just like phrase drill in mechanics. Drill with digits is useful to sharpen recognition of details because one number has no relation to another. Start working with three-digit numbers, advance to four and keep stepping up the number of digits until you reach eight. Columns of numbers in the telephone book provide excellent practice.

234	4961	87142	3498781	9–2226
521	7387	13 65	8143223	3–3814
517	3718	27721	563 819	4–6259
452	6942	30975	7201287	7–6536
908	1963	717844	94784323	5–0275
704	24712	426791	46417419	2–3677
127	598 2	176791	20254917	1–0041
839	41632	940918	64784934	3–9818

Be as tough as you can when you flash the card. Pull it down and up with the shortest possible exposure. You are the only person who is going to know your score, so don't try to cheat. This is excellent training in faster reading.

Your target here is to decrease the amount of time it takes

your eyes to photograph an image and transmit it to your mind. Later on I shall be talking about the importance of vocabulary in the rapid-reading score. I'll preview that here only to say that words — like faces — are images. Their conformation tends to make recognition easy. The bigger the vocabulary, the quicker you recognize words. The more words you know, the faster you can read. Particularly in flash reading, a small vocabulary is a heavy handicap to reading speed.

Space Reading

In rapid reading one aid is to focus the eyes just above the words rather than on the line itself. This gives a sort of perspective which tends to make the words stand out in phrases. You absorb and photograph them more quickly. It is the same principle sailors are taught in looking for another ship or a landmark at night. Focus just to one side of where you think the object must be. Then you see it quickly.

Pacing in Regular Reading

After you have worked with the newspaper a while and practiced the other exercises, I want you to spend an evening reading a fairly light novel. It should be something that isn't difficult. Use a Pacing Card. Place it so that it just covers the top line on each page. Draw it down in even rhythm over the lines, always a little faster than you can comfortably read. Try to feel the pace. Then put aside the card and go on reading in the same rhythm. Do not, under any circumstances, let your eyes regress. If you miss something, forget it. Just read and read and read — as fast as you can.

If you have been working steadily on the techniques I have shown you, you will finish the book in an evening. You may have spent a week on a novel before but when you go to bed tonight you have turned the last page. This is the first triumph and dividend I can offer you from your Modern Reading course. You have read an entire book in a single evening!

Well, get a stack of paperbacks. You will need them, because one of the requirements of Modern Reading is to keep yourself alert by constant practice. Whenever you have a free evening at home, pick up the next paperback. Use the card to pace yourself down the first 20 pages. Then cut loose and continue reading at speed. Concentrate! Read in phrases! Use all the skills! Now you know that faster reading isn't just a theory. It works for *you!*

Fifth Day: Skipping and Skimming

THESE TWO TIMESAVERS, skipping and skimming, grow directly out of pre-reading, and we had better start by defining them. *Skipping* means simply that, on the basis of pre-reading, you jump over large sections of material. When you *skim* you cast your eyes down a page of type without actually reading but looking for significant phrases or important facts to stop you. You saw in pre-reading that you skipped a great deal but still got the main drift. As an efficient reader you will often *skip* passages — to save time and because these have nothing new. You will often *skim* for facts or ideas.

Of course untrained readers skip and skim too. But their trouble is that they do it in a haphazard manner — because they are not fully aware of the *purpose* for which they are reading. Their minds are not engaged, so even the parts they skim fail to produce information.

The trained reader, on the other hand, knows exactly why he is reading at all times. He concentrates on everything he looks at and is therefore alert to recognize whether it has value for him. He accepts skipping and skimming as the useful tools they are and makes them serve their proper purposes of saving time and helping him to find quickly some fact he is looking for.

In discussing skipping and skimming I am considering

these skills almost entirely as they apply in reading information material. You will use them also in pleasure reading at times — when descriptive or expository passages seem overlong, when slow-moving action fails to hold your interest. But that is so much a matter of personal reaction and reading preference that no generalizations apply. I will hazard a guess, nevertheless, that as your reading speed increases you will skip less and less when your purpose is straight enjoyment. Your reading will have become so effortless that skipping seems hardly worthwhile. Because you are concentrating and your mind is involved, sections that might have bored you before now seem to be filled with interest. You read them eagerly, enjoying the author's style.

But with information reading, skipping and skimming are necessary to carry you through the mass of material which engulfs you at times. Let's see now exactly how these two skills serve the efficient reader.

Skipping

Few people know how to skip with confidence because most people do not pre-read. Yet pre-reading is the guide, since it is the one way to acquaint yourself with what an article or book contains and therefore how much of it you ought to read. You are already doing considerable skipping as you pre-read. But you now know what a book or article has to offer. You have a good idea of the parts you should read thoroughly as well as those you can skip without much danger of missing anything.

Skipping is simply selection. When you are reading an article for a certain kind of information, and the author turns to a part of his subject which doesn't concern you — skip until he comes back. Unless tables of figures and statistics are worth remembering — skip confidently. You'll know where to find them for reference later. The author needed them to prove his point. But you needn't study them in detail if you are willing to take the author's word that his documentation is sound. Skip detailed technical explanations unless they apply to your own specialized field. Be alert for passages in which an author repeats for emphasis a point he has already made. He is "saying it in a different way," and the chances are you don't care.

To sum up, pre-reading provides a guide to parts of an article which you should skip. But a quick survey cannot always show up irrelevant passages which may also be skipped, even though you had planned on thorough reading. Skipping serves you best when, with the full concentration you have learned to apply, you are quick to scent paragraphs or whole sections which do not carry out their first promise and have no information that you care about having for your present reading purpose — or do not already know.

Skimming

Skimming is simply the process of casting your eyes quickly over an article. But again, unless you have a *purpose*, you will get very little benefit. There are just two reasons for skimming: 1. To find a specific piece of information which you know the article contains. 2. To hunt on the chance you will stumble on significant phrases or stray facts you can use. These have a way of jumping out at you in purposeful skimming. But you must know what you are looking for.

Skimming for a fact. You are looking for a fact —let's say it is the date of the 1960 Presidential election. You are reasonably sure it is somewhere in the article you have before you. You don't want to read the article. You just want that elusive date.

Here's how to find it quickly. Let your eyes travel down the page without actually reading, stopping twice on each line of type. A good way to practice is to lay a pencil vertically on the center of the page or column. Let your eyes make two fixations at first on each line — one to the left and one to the right of the pencil.

Practice Skimming

When you're skimming for spe-

cific information, either for a fact or

for the answer to a question, don't

let your attention wander. Keep in

mind exactly what it is you are look-

ing for. As you improve your skill

you will find that the date, name or

phrase jumps out of the page. And

by the way, here's that date you

were after — November 8, 1960.

Don't look directly at the type. Look just above it — at the white space between the lines. After you have followed this eye-swing pattern for a few lines, start letting your eyes make just one fixation on each line. Beginning with line 7, fixate to the left of the pencil, and on line 8 fixate to the right. Make these zig-zag fixations on succeeding lines until you find the date you were looking for.

When you are skimming for a specific fact, don't let your

attention wander. Keep in mind exactly what it is you are looking for. As you improve your skill with practice you will find that the date, name or phrase actually seems to jump out of the page. And here, by the way, is that date you were after — November 8, 1960.

Skimming for chance facts and phrases. This second skimming technique is useful whenever you are doubtful that an article has anything to serve your purpose but want to make sure in the shortest possible time. You can use skimming during pre-reading, if you wish. When you begin to read first sentences of paragraphs only in pre-reading (see Chapter One), try skimming the remainder of the paragraphs quickly, looking for names, dates and significant phrases you may want to remember. Focus just above the lines of type and let your eyes zig-zag back and forth. What you need to see will jump out at you.

It will, that is, if you know what you are looking for. That is the important thing when you skim. Just as you must read with a purpose, so you must skim with a purpose. Otherwise, as your eyes wander down the page your mind will begin to wander too. You will keep your mind glued firmly to its task if you are concentrating and following the pre-reading pattern of reading the first sentence of every paragraph and skimming for facts and phrases in between.

The researchers I mentioned in Chapter One will find skimming an invaluable skill to cultivate. It is a miraculous timesaver when you must look through a great many books and articles related to your subject but not necessarily directly concerned with the aspect you expect to write about. By skimming, along with pre-reading, the researcher can usually make up his mind quickly whether a particular item is worth pursuing. And skimming is a wonderful short cut in chasing down a fact or a date which is bound to be somewhere in a certain book chapter.

How to Test Yourself

As you begin the practice of skipping and skimming with a purpose you should test yourself frequently. Here are the steps to follow:

1. Pre-read an article, skipping parts and skimming the rest.

2. Write a one-paragraph summary of the author's theme and main ideas.

3. Go back and read the article thoroughly. Write a second brief summary, without looking at the first.

When you compare the two, do you find that you put down vital facts the second time which show that your first summary was inadequate or even incorrect? If this happens, you are not yet sufficiently skillful at picking out important ideas when you skim, or not selective enough in what you choose to skip. This means you need more concentrated practice on these two skills until you are confident you have mastered them.

CHAPTER SIX

Sixth Day: Vocabulary—I

To READ RAPIDLY you must instantly recognize thousands of words. You have probably discovered already in doing some of the practice drills that failure to know a word puts a power brake on your speed. The only way to overcome this handicap is to add constantly to the reservoir of words at your command.

In a short book like this it is impossible to go into specific exercises designed to increase your store of words. You will find excellent manuals on vocabulary building in the paperbacks. Buy one and study it at the same time you are working on rapid reading.

I also suggest that you get a special notebook in which you write down unfamiliar words. Don't stop to look up words while you are reading. When you have finished is the time for a session with the dictionary. You will retain the word better if you copy the definition and put the word immediately in a sentence. It's a good idea to review new words regularly till you are sure you have mastered them.

Now let's consider this matter of vocabulary, and it would be a good idea for you to do a little self-searching on the state of your present familiarity with words. As you learned in the Introduction, every person has three types of vocabulary:

1. Active. These are the words you customarily use in speaking. Your active vocabulary probably runs from 5,000 to 10,000 words.

2. Reserve. These are the words you know but rarely if ever use in ordinary speech. You use them in writing a letter, when you have more time to consider or when you are searching for a synonym. You know these words well enough so that you would not hesitate over them in rapid reading.

3. Passive. This is the odds and ends residue of words that you recognize vaguely but are not sure of the meanings. You never use them in either speech or writing. You just know that you have seen them before, and they'll stop you dead in rapid reading.

To increase the size of your vocabulary you should constantly upgrade words until they are part of your active vocabulary, ready for use when an occasion rises. If you work at this, you will be pleasantly surprised at the words you begin to use. Even quite unfamiliar words may find their way into your conversation. As an example, the recent craze for dinosaurs brought dozens of forbidding-looking words into the vocabularies of youngsters fascinated by the great prehistoric reptiles. You may never have known the Latin names — and there are no common ones — of such beasts as tyrannosaurus rex, stegosaurus, triceratops, brontosaurus, pterodactyl, archeopteryx. But if your children started producing dinosaurs from the make-it-yourself kits you had to learn the words to keep on speaking terms.

The sudden opening of the space age pushed a good many new and difficult words out of the science laboratories and into everyday conversation. To pick another example, the appearance of plastics as a household commonplace in clothing materials and kitchenware also contributed many new words to the language.

If you get the dictionary and notebook habit, it will put both color and accuracy into your every-day speech. When you know the precise meanings of all the words in your passive vocabulary now, you will find that you speak with more assurance and without the sort of painful, awkward, round-about sentence structure which a meagre vocabulary makes necessary for the person who does not know the words which would express his ideas with exactitude. Don't be timid with words.

How the Newspaper Helps

Your newspaper is a ready means of building vocabulary, and in a later chapter I shall explain in detail how you can use it to fullest advantage. Since you presumably read a newspaper every day, make it pay off for you right now by adding new words to your store. Newspapers are designed for quick reading, but this doesn't mean that all the words are simple and familiar. In its daily job the newspaper covers many kinds of events. It describes them with the words best suited to tell the story briefly and clearly.

From a single issue of a newspaper I collected a list of 30 words. They are not difficult, but see if you can recognize and define each with confidence. If you can't, look it up. These are all accurate representations of ideas which in most cases would require several words to express differently.

agenda	derogatory	expunge	lenient	protocol
avaricious	dinghy	facet	megaton	rescind
coalition	disillusion	fantasy	moratorium	scourge
cognizant	dispossess	ideological	motivate	seismic
contemporary	embargo	incongruous	opulence	venerable
decade	evasion	indicted	posthumously	zealous

If you will note down a few unfamiliar words each day from your newspaper your vocabulary will begin to grow and flower.

Prefixes and Suffixes

One quick aid to vocabulary building is knowing the prefixes and suffixes from which many words are built. Mastering their meanings will help to increase your reading speed too. It opens the door to what I call *intelligent anticipation*, a tool all rapid readers learn to use. A grasp of the familiar prefixes will get you into a word quickly; a knowledge of the suffixes will get you out of it, since you anticipate what the rest of the word *must* be from the shape of the ending.

The modern English language contains many words taken over from other countries. Often good English words are made up of parts borrowed from other languages. The prefixes and suffixes come chiefly from Greek and Latin and they usually appear in English with the original meaning intact. This gives an immediate clue to what the word you are about to read will mean. It may suggest a certain kind of action: *out, off, away from, down, up, around.* Or it will warn you that the word is going to have a meaning *characteristic of,* or *relating to,* or *belonging to.* Suffixes often express the same kinds of relations or actions.

Let's take two words apart to see how this works:

The prefix *amphi-* is Greek, and one of its meanings is "of two or both kinds." *Bios* is also a Greek word and means "life." Put them together in "amphibious" and you have an animal that has two lives — in the water and on land. Or, as "amphibian," the word means an airplane that will take off and land on either the ground or the water.

Now a suffix, *-able.* This is such straight English that it seems unnecessary to remember its Latin origin as *-abilis.* Anyway, the meaning is obvious when you add it to such a stem as "love." "Lovable" means simply worthy to be loved. All the "ables" have the meaning of *able to, capable of, worthy of, having qualities of, leaning toward,* etc.

Here are 20 common prefixes and 20 suffixes to start you out:

Prefixes. ambi-, an-, anti-, apo-, bi-, com-, di-, hemi-, hyper-, hypo-, in-, meta-, mono-, para-, peri-, poly-, pre-, pro-, syn-, trans-.

Suffixes. -able, -acy, -age, -ance, -arium,- ary, -en, -esque, -gamy, -ic, -ine, -ist, -ity, -logy, -ly, -ment, -oid, -ous, -tion, -tude.

Copy these down and learn their definitions. You will find them all and others in any of the several fine desk dictionaries available — and everyone studying Modern Reading *must* have such a dictionary. Prefixes and suffixes are listed in their proper alphabetical order as though they were complete words — that is, "-tion" follows "tiny."

Children are taught simple sums in addition, subtraction and multiplication as "arithmetic facts" to remember. Much of the drudgery of doing problems is taken away when they have mastered these "facts." Prefixes and suffixes are "reading facts." Knowing their meanings gives you a head start in quick perception (and that word carries both a prefix and a suffix, you will notice).

A bigger vocabulary plus these reading facts will speed your *perception rate.* This is simply the time required for your mind to recognize words from the images the eyes flash to it. Speeding up your perception rate leads to faster reading, since it cuts down the time required to absorb a word. That is why a wide vocabulary is so necessary to the rapid reader.

Don't stop just with adding words you have never seen before. Make sure you clear up doubts about words only half understood now. Then use them, say them in conversation. Don't be timid. Speak up! This growing articulateness will make you more *sure* as you read that you have got the full sense of what the author was saying. As your word knowledge builds confidence, your comprehension builds with it.

CHAPTER SEVEN

Seventh Day: Pacing

O NE POPULAR MISCONCEPTION of rapid reading is that when a person learns to read at high speed he will race through everything at this accelerated pace. Don't believe it. No one expects you to read a scientific article filled with unfamiliar technical words, or a book of poems, at the same speed with which you properly gallop through a mystery novel.

This is no more than common sense. Think back to the analogy of the automobile I cited in the Introduction. I suppose a man *could* drive his car at 60 miles an hour over a curving mountain road. But he would be pretty uncomfortable and he wouldn't take in much of the scenery. So he slows down to a sensible pace which permits him to enjoy driving and gives him a chance to look across the valleys on both sides of his mountain road.

In the same way, once you have learned to read rapidly you *could* romp through anything. But if the material is new, the words and ideas unfamiliar, you wouldn't do so with the comprehension which makes high speed worth while. And if the selection was a piece of fine writing you wouldn't have time to appreciate its beauty. You are now reading everything at a much faster rate than you did before you began to practice Modern Reading. You will never go back to the snail's pace you followed before you discovered the pleasures of this better method. But you will not read everything at your maximum speed. You will now be a many-gaited reader, adjusting your speed to the kind of reading you are doing at the moment.

In a general way, everything you read falls into four categories and, in keeping with the principles of Modern Reading, these divisions are based on the several *purposes* which decide you to read. Here they are: 1. *For information only*. 2. *To evaluate and criticize ideas*. 3. *For self-enrichment*. 4. *For relaxation and enjoyment*.

Quite obviously there will be a certain amount of overlapping of purpose within these categories. But the reader who keeps them in mind and stops to fix the purpose of his reading will find his grasp of new material is greatly accelerated and also his enjoyment, since he has adjusted both his point of view and his speed in advance. Now let's see what different kinds of material fall into each category:

1. For information only. This is a high-speed category. Reports, business letters, technical articles in your field go in first. Sessions with an encyclopedia or reference book are included and, of course, all the textbooks that students use. You want information but you don't particularly care about the quality of the writing as long as it is clear. You read just as fast as your comprehension will permit, skipping and skimming when these techniques seem safe to use. The strictly news reports in your newspaper fall into this category too, though you will probably slow down for special articles and editorials which require the more critical approach of category two.

2. To evaluate and criticize ideas. This calls for slower speed. The category contains books and other writing in which the author is presenting a point of view. The alert reader does not simply accept what is written but brings his own background knowledge and intelligence to bear in an evaluation of the author's discussion and conclusions. He asks questions as he goes along, trying to anticipate points as the argument develops. This process increases enormously the reader's enjoyment of such material. His mind is completely involved, his concentration fully applied. If your own mind has been only half alive with this kind of material before, applying the principles of Modern Reading will increase your appreciation in great measure. For this is more than just a skill. You will find that it unfolds a whole new dimension of understanding because you are gearing yourself to evaluate the opinions of the great thinkers of today and yesterday. You now read more easily, more rapidly, so your mind is able to absorb ideas quickly and concern itself with estimating their logic.

If you ever learned to play a musical instrument, you reached a point where the fingering — the simple technique — could be forgotten. You could play without thinking of the mechanics. Now you could devote yourself to an *interpretation* of music. It is the same with Modern Reading. You reach a point where you are no longer concerned with each technique of reading. You can lose yourself in what the author is saying, argue with him, criticize his conclusions.

I am not sure you have reached this point yet, unless you have an exceptional aptitude. You are still concerned with drills and practice. But at least you know the goal that lies ahead. It is the point at which you use Modern Reading principles naturally.

3. For self-enrichment. When you read with this purpose you expect not only the beauty of fine writing but of inspiring thoughts. Great novels find their place here, great plays and poetry, richly conceived and written biographies, history, philosophy and the other humanities. Sometimes the

PART ONE. READ FASTER

writing will be difficult. Sometimes it will flow easily into your
mind. There is always an overflow from category two into this
kind of writing, but here you are not so alive to criticism. Only
when the author's thoughts or interpretations clash with your
own background knowledge will you find yourself questioning,
arguing with him in your mind. For the most part, this kind
of reading experience is something which brings only pleasure
to your mind and awakens your imagination.

You will not want to read memorable writing at your top
pace. But as your general reading skill increases you will
handle this kind of material far more rapidly than you do today
and without sacrifice of the self-enrichment it promises. This
is where your growing vocabulary counts most. There are no
holds barred in words an author may use in a biography or fine
novel. He will not set out deliberately to stump you with
difficult words. But if one occurs to him as exactly the right
expression of a thought or emotion he will not hesitate to use
it. With material of this sort the advice about vocabulary
building in the previous chapter pays big dividends.

4. For relaxation and enjoyment. Now you are settling down for a pleasant evening with one of those paperbacks
I mentioned (and it can be a hardbound book just as well). It
will be a light novel, a detective story, an absorbing true
adventure, a piece of humor, a funny biography. This is where
rapid reading comes into its own, for you should race through
such material at top speed. The writing is adequate for the
purpose but it is not great. You will not want to pause over it.
You are simply absorbing mood and situation.

How to Fix Your Pace

Once you have these four categories in your mind
and can establish a purpose each time you read you will
want to ask, "But just how do I fix my speed with different

kinds of material? Is there some rule of thumb I can learn?"

No, there is no rule of thumb, but there are practical realities which guide you. The questions apply most directly to the second and third categories — in reading to evaluate and criticize ideas and in reading for self-enrichment. I have already made clear that when you are reading for information only — "practical prose," this sort of thing is usually called — or when you are reading purely for relaxation and enjoyment you race along at top speed.

Now let's consider speed in the second category. The reason no general rule can be offered is that each person approaches critical reading with a different fund of knowledge. This, in turn, governs the difficulty of a particular piece of writing — *for him.*

An EXAMPLE will help to illustrate the point: You are a businessman with average intellectual background. You are interested in foreign affairs but no expert. A new crisis erupts somewhere in the world. You have read about it in your newspaper and now you come across a solid article in one of the monthly magazines. You decide to read it, and your purpose will be not only to get information but to evaluate and criticize the author's views. You pre-read of course but you find you must slow down when you start to read the article thoroughly. There will be unfamiliar names of officials, place names you recall only vaguely. You will probably run across statistics on the country's economic situation, talk of clashing political parties. For *you*, because most of the material is new, this is not easy going.

Now take another man whose intellectual equipment is no better than your own but who has spent some time in the troubled country. He has a head start in background and should be able to read the same article at faster speed because his comprehension is already primed. He knows what he is reading about.

The guide to pacing yourself on material in this category is your comprehension rate. You read as rapidly as you can without missing anything of importance. To test your progress it is well to time yourself on serious articles and keep a running score. The best way to check comprehension rate is to skim an article immediately after you read it, making sure that you have retained all the main points.

One warning: Do not feel discouraged if your speed falls off now and then, even with articles on subjects that are *familiar* to you. An author's style has a great deal to do with your ease of comprehension. Some experts are unable to write clearly and simply. Their sentence structure becomes involved and their meaning tangled up in a confused web of jargon and dependent clauses. A better writer could have stated the same facts and opinions so that you would slide through his article rapidly. But he might lack the expert's authority.

Your pace will always be slowest in this second category since you will be asking questions while you read. As your general speed and skill increase, you will quicken your gait here too. So stretch yourself as much as you can — but not at the sacrifice of comprehension. The speed will come.

And now how about reading for self-enrichment? How do you pace yourself when you want to appreciate sheer beauty of writing and nobility of phrase? "I *want* to read this kind of writing slowly," you insist. But you don't — not really. The reason goes back to a point I made in Chapter Two. When you read slowly it is hard to keep your mind engaged, for the full richness of phrase and sentence is not coming in fast enough. It is like looking at the individual pieces in a beautiful stained-glass window rather than at the entire luminous image.

To be sure, you will read fine prose more slowly than you would a mystery story. But you should still strive for speed instead of deliberately holding back. When you are able to absorb a good biography at a far faster pace than you can right now your appreciation of the style will be increased rather than diminished. You will feel that you are getting the picture whole rather than in bits and pieces.

Do not hesitate to use the Pacing Card with this kind of material, drawing it smoothly down the lines in consistent rhythm and a little faster than is quite comfortable. This helps to establish your gait. And don't worry about missing beauty. You'll find it just where it should be — transferred from the pages to your mind and your memory.

Timing Test for Self-enrichment

At this point in your progress, I think you would be interested to try your speed on a passage to be read for self-enrichment. I have chosen one of the minor classics — the beginning of Robert Louis Stevenson's essay, "On Falling in Love," from the series called "Virginibus Puerisque." These essays are often used as school assignments, so quite possibly you have read this before. Now try it again with your new skills and see how fast you can go without missing any of Stevenson's nice turn of phrase and gentle humor. Don't look back if you feel you have lost some of the meaning. Read the excerpt straight through. But if you know you are missing a great deal, this is the signal to slow down to an even pace with which comprehension can keep up.

To test your comprehension, after you have finished the passage write a hundred-word summary of what Stevenson says. This is the best means I know of finding out just how much of an author's thought a person has absorbed.

Starting Time: _____ **MINUTES** _____ **SECONDS**

Begin Timing:

There is only one event in life which really astonishes a man and startles him out of his prepared opinions. Everything else befalls him very much as he expected. Event succeeds to event, with an agreeable variety indeed, but with little that is either startling or intense; they form together no more than a sort of background, or running accompaniment to the man's own reflections; and he falls naturally into a cool, curious and smiling habit of mind, and builds himself up in a conception of life which expects tomorrow to be after the pattern of today and yesterday. . .

There is probably nothing rightly thought or rightly written on the matter of love that is not a piece of the person's experience. I remember an anecdote of a well-known French theorist, who was debating a point eagerly in a circle of friends. It was objected against him that he had never experienced love. Whereupon he arose, left the society, and made it a point not to return to it until he considered that he had supplied the defect.

"Now," he remarked, on entering, "now I am in a position to continue the discussion." Perhaps he had not penetrated very deeply into the subject after all; but the story indicates right thinking, and may serve as an apologue to readers of this essay.

When at last the scales fall from his eyes, it is not without something of the nature of dismay that the man finds himself in such changed conditions. He has to deal with commanding emotions instead of the easy dislikes and preferences in which he has hitherto passed his days; and he recognizes capabilities for pain and pleasure of which he had not yet suspected the existence.

Falling in love is the one illogical adventure, the one thing of which we are tempted to think as supernatural, in our trite and reasonable world. The effect is out of all proportion with the cause. Two persons, neither of them, it may be, very amiable or very beautiful, meet, speak a little, and look a little into each other's eyes. That has been done a dozen or so of times in the experience of either with no great result. But on this occasion all is different. They fall at once into that state in which another person becomes to us the very gist and center-point of God's creation, and demolishes our laborious theories with a smile; in which our ideas are so bound up with the one master-thought that even the trivial cares of our own person become so many acts of devotion, and the love of life itself is translated into a wish to remain in the same world with so precious and desirable a fellow creature.

And all the while their acquaintances look on in stupor, and ask each other, with almost passionate emphasis, what so-and-so can see in that woman, or such-an-one in that man? I am sure, gentlemen, I cannot tell you. For my part, I cannot think what the women mean. It might be very well, if the Apollo Belvedere should suddenly glow all over into life, and step forward from the pedestal with that godlike air of his. But of the misbegotten changelings who call themselves men, and prate intolerably over dinner tables, I never saw one who seemed worthy to inspire love — no, nor read of any, except Leonardo da Vinci, and perhaps Goethe in his youth. About women I entertain a somewhat different opinion; but there, I have the misfortune to be a man.

Stop Timing

Finish time ———— **MINUTES** ———— **SECONDS**

About 680 words   **READING TIME**————

Find your reading score by the chart, page 8, or by the equation I have given you. Set it down below:

———— wpm

CHAPTER EIGHT

Review of Part One

You have now been shown both the basic concepts and the steps to faster reading. When you start Part Two you are moving toward a higher plateau of enjoyment where you will learn to become a *better* reader as well as a *faster* one. But first I should like to give you a practice program to follow until you are confident that *all* the skills are working for you *all the time*. The *Schedule of Drills* puts you through a daily review of what you have been shown in Part One.

If you are like most people, you do not use the techniques naturally as yet. You have to remind yourself whenever you pick up a newspaper, a book or a magazine to put the skills into practice. After a while, they should become an instinctive and almost unconscious part of your reading attitude. But this will happen only if you practice regularly. The important thing is to establish a routine whereby you make certain that you use *all* of the techniques of faster reading. It is not necessary to make a study period of this. You will absorb the method most naturally if you apply the techniques in the course of a normal day's reading. The *Schedule of Drills* is simply a handy checklist to make sure you are doing them all. Here it is:

Schedule of Drills

1. Pre-reading (Chapter One). Pre-read an article. Whether you read it thoroughly afterward is unimportant. What *is* important in this exercise is to *make the decision:* "I should read it," or, "I don't need to." Pre-reading trains you to make up your mind quickly whether to spend time reading further. Always pre-read as fast as you can, following the method explained in Chapter One.

2. Phrase reading (Chapter Two). Several important drills help you to read in phrases: *a.* Work at widening your *span of recognition* by trying to increase the number of words you see at each *fixation.* Practicing the "eye-swing" exercise (page 30) will quicken this skill. *b.* Train yourself not to look at the extreme left of a line but at the second word. This gives a lead in cutting down fixations. Lifting your eyes before the end of the line has the same effect. *c.* Circling *units of meaning* in newspaper articles will help you become conscious of phrases and so let your mind absorb ideas faster. *d.* Separating *units of meaning* with a pencil/ by diagonal bars/ like this/ is less clumsy/. You will/ find this/ is good drill/ for comprehension too/. *e.* Fixing your eyes *just above* a line of type as you read helps make phrases stand out.

3. Concentration (Chapter Three). This is something you can practice anywhere, and your own will power is the key. You must fight against letting distracting noises interfere with your absorption in reading; you must force your emotional problems into the background. It requires intelligence and persistence to achieve concentration. But it must be done if you are to read rapidly with full comprehension. With continued practice you should find that your reading becomes more important than what is going on around you.

4. Speed Drills (Chapter Four). Each of the drills described in Chapter Four should be practiced daily. Here they are: *a. Columnar reading:* Fix your eyes on the center of a newspaper column, draw them down the column rapidly, trying to see as many words as possible on both sides. *b. Stretch your speed* by drawing a Pacing Card down the pages of a book a little faster than you can comfortably read. Put aside the Pacing Card and go on reading at the same speed. *c.* To quicken perception, use the *flash-card* technique on columns of phrases and digits. (See Chapter Four for details.)

5. Skipping and skimming (Chapter Five). To practice *skipping*, read an article rapidly, trying to get the author's main points, but skipping long explanations and what seems irrelevant. Then read the article thoroughly and see how much you missed that was really important. For efficient *skimming* you must know in advance what you are looking for — facts, dates, significant phrases, details of a certain sort. By pre-reading any article you know what you may expect to find. Set your purpose and start skimming. If you have an encyclopedia, this provides excellent drill. Pick out the name of any person. Decide on half-a-dozen facts to find — dates of his birth and death and place of each. The maiden name of his wife, where he lived most of his life, the principal distinction he reached. Now lay a pencil vertically down the center of the column and skim, swinging your eyes from left to right and back.

6. Vocabulary Building (Chapter Six). Add at least eight or ten words each day to your notebook of unfamiliar words. Upgrade words in your *reserve* and *passive* vocabularies and use them in conversation. Look up all words you are not sure of in the dictionary, write down definitions and make sentences using each one. Above all things, study the pronunciation of unfamiliar words and *say them aloud*. You never really know a word until you are on speaking terms with it. In daily newspaper reading make it a point to circle all unfamiliar words and look them up later in the dictionary. Your vocabulary will be enormously enriched with expressions that are alive and part of today's living language. Study prefixes and suffixes. Knowing them thoroughly will greatly increase your *perception rate*. These prefixes and suffixes are *reading facts* which should always lie on the rim of the mind.

7. Pacing (Chapter Seven). If you have not already learned the four general categories of reading material described in Chapter Seven you should do so now. They are basic in deciding your reading *purpose* and so will serve as a guide in fixing your speed. The speed at which a person reads in the two slower categories — reading to evaluate and criticize ideas, reading for self-enrichment — depends directly on his background of knowledge and therefore his ability to comprehend. Reading speed will vary widely with different individuals on the same selection. The drill is to stretch yourself constantly by reading just a little faster than is comfortable but at which comprehension keeps pace with speed. Using the Pacing Card at times will help you to read evenly, and this is important. Do not slow below the rate at which your comprehension keeps pace. Now that you are reading everything more rapidly you can probably handle difficult material faster than you may believe. Don't be afraid of it.

PART TWO

Read Better

The Rewards of Better Reading

FASTER READING, useful as it is with routine information material, is not an end in itself. It is only the gateway to *better reading*. The skills developed in Part One of this book are designed to overcome handicaps which keep most untrained readers from the pleasures of stretching their knowledge. In Part Two you move ahead to achieve the rewards of better reading.

But even as it is, your training in faster reading so far has geared you to enjoy reading a great deal more and to read with greater intelligence. If you have worked conscientiously, there have been four major advances in your reading facility. Here they are:

1. *Rapid reading* has waked up both eyes and mind to receive images and ideas quickly and clearly.
2. *Concentration* now keeps attention from wandering. Your mind is fully engaged by what you read.
3. An expanded *vocabulary* now helps you recognize and understand many more words than you did before.
4. *Pacing* your reading speed to suit different kinds of material helps develop *comprehension*.

The Program of Part Two

You are now going to consolidate these advances. The rewards ahead develop progressively, one from the other, just as did the skills of the Seven Days to Faster Reading. These are the real goals you have been working toward. There are five:

1. You will train yourself to remember or "retain" more easily — to *retain* what you read and store it away as a new part of your background knowledge — to be drawn on in future reading experiences.

2. Better *retention* produces better comprehension. The information, ideas and points of view you are constantly acquiring become an ever-widening base on which comprehension depends.

3. Broader *comprehension*, in turn, leads to greater skill in handling critical material — that is to say, the articles and books which express opinions and views that can be controversial. You will want to weigh this kind of material before you accept or reject the views.

4. These advanced reading skills force you to stretch your vocabulary constantly as you encounter unfamiliar words. Chapter Ten gives you a new method of increasing word recognition through the use of your newspaper.

5. Finally, the biggest reward of all is the one you give to yourself through vastly increased reading in many fields.

This is the program laid out in Part Two, and you will be following it all your life. I do not mean practicing drills and exercises as such. When you finish the book, the techniques should be a part of you which you will use always to stretch yourself in the new knowledge and enjoyment you gain from books and other reading through this faster and better way.

By acquiring the full skill of better reading you will awaken a fresh curiosity to learn. If you are past thirty you may think you had lost the hunger for learning years ago. Most such people have left it dormant only because heavy reading seemed such a chore. With new skill the urge quickly returns. For young people in high school and college, advanced reading facility sharply increases the desire to learn. At any age better reading stimulates the appetite. There is a rich pride of accomplishment in the assurance that you are an expert reader.

People sometimes ask me if their new facility is permanent. "Will I lose my speed if I don't practice exercises constantly?" From my own experience in the Reading Laboratory with thousands of individuals I can answer confidently that you will not lose your speed once these techniques are wholly a part of you — as long as you keep on reading. For in the very act of reading you *do* practice. In everything you read the skills are at work. The answer is really as simple as that.

IN PART TWO you will find more tests, but by now you should also be reading books on your own. As you do, keep on timing yourself. Since you will now be reading for long periods and over many pages, you will not need to use the chart on page 8 or the timing technique explained in the Introduction to Part One for short exercises in which seconds are important. You will need a pencil and paper now to do some simple mathematics. Here are the steps in these longer reading sessions:

1. You don't need to count every word you read. You count the pages, and your first chore is to find the average number of words on each. To do this, count the number of words in each of 12 or 15 lines anywhere in your book. Find the average

number of words per line. Say it works out to be 11.

2. Now count the number of lines of type on a full page of text. Suppose it is 35. Multiply 11 × 35, and this will give the average number of words on a page — 385.

3. Now multiply 385 by the number of pages you covered and divide the answer by the number of minutes you read. For example, you read 100 pages of 385 words in one hour and 20 minutes — — 38,500 words in 80 minutes. Divide 38,500 by 80 to find your speed — 482 words a minute.

To be quite realistic in your progress, it is a good idea to keep a notebook which not only preserves a running record of reading speed but notes down the sort of material you were reading. Always remember that speed will — and *should* — vary with different kinds of reading. If you read a mystery novel last night at 670 words a minute and a biography tonight at 425, do not think that you are losing ground. The variation is simply the result of pacing *speed* to *comprehension*. As time goes on, you should increase that rate of 425 words on the biography, but your score on this kind of material will always be slower than on light reading.

After a while, you will no longer be concerned with speed per minute. It is fun to figure now — and don't miss any of the satisfaction a faster word count brings. When you have consolidated all the skills so that you use them quite unconsciously your pleasure will grow out of the assurance that you are reading much more rapidly — with full comprehension — whatever the material happens to be.

That sort of heightened skill is what you are working toward now as you begin Part Two.

CHAPTER NINE

Retention

THE MIND is a film which retains everything that is printed on it through sight and the other senses. Obviously, in reading, the images perceived most intensively are those the mind retains best. Some people say, "My mind is a sieve. Everything slips through it. I never can remember anything I read."

This is because they aren't trying. Their attention is scattered over a dozen different diversions. To retain what you read it is necessary to follow a certain discipline. It grows naturally out of the Seven Days to Faster Reading.

Here it is:

1. You must be sufficiently interested in what you read to *want* to remember its *important facts*. Unless you concentrate, the images will not register clearly enough to be easily recalled.

2. You must drill yourself to distinguish important facts from details you can disregard.

3. You must be constantly alert to keep the direction of the author's thought running actively in your mind.

Two techniques will help you to develop *retention* as a skill.

The first is recognizing *key words*. The second is *summarizing* paragraphs mentally as you go along.

1. Key words. In all writing the sense of paragraphs is carried along in key words. Sentences contain many unimportant words and phrases to fill out the style — to make pleasant, imaginative prose. Unless you are reading simply to enjoy the style, retention is quickened by jumping from key word to key word. This takes some practice but it isn't a difficult skill.

To illustrate, here is a paragraph from a famous letter Benjamin Franklin wrote to Madame Brillon, one of the great court ladies, when he was our agent in France in 1779. As "The Whistle," the letter has been reprinted in many anthologies. Here is the incident that inspired it:

"When I was a child of seven years old my friends on a holiday filled my pocket with coppers. I went directly to a shop where they sold toys for children, and being charmed with the sound of a whistle that I met by the way in the hands of another boy, I voluntarily offered and gave all my money for one. I then came home and went whistling all over the house, much pleased with my whistle, but disturbing all the family. My brothers and sisters and cousins, understanding the bargain I had made, told me I had given four times as much for it as it was worth, put me in mind what good things I might have bought with the rest of the money, and laughed at me so much for my folly that I cried with vexation; and the reflection gave me more chagrin than the whistle gave me pleasure."

Without meaning to do violence to Ben Franklin's pleasant style, here are the key words which carry the sense of the entire paragraph:

"When I was   seven   friends   filled my pocket with
coppers. I went   shop   toys,   being charmed   sound
of a whistle   met by the way   another boy   voluntarily
offered   all my money for one.   came home   whistling all
over the house   My brothers and sisters told me   given
four times   it was worth   what good things   bought with
rest of money   laughed at   my folly   I cried;   gave me
more chagrin than   whistle gave   pleasure."

In this kind of reading for key words you do not skip the
words between but you brush over them lightly so that the *key
words* register sharply and retain the sense for you. If you
remember the key words in the Franklin selection you can easily
reconstruct the story in the paragraph long after you read it.

2. Summarizing.
A second technique which is a powerful
aid to retention is to summarize paragraphs in your mind as
you go along. It may seem at first that this is bound to put a
brake on speed. If you stopped to write down summaries of
course it would. But you don't. When you have practiced
mental summarizing for a while, under full concentration, a
sort of after-image of the paragraph remains with you, even as
you are going ahead at high speed. If you become conscious
of this after-image you will retain the main ideas and keep the
sequence of the author's discussion flowing as you read.

To see how well you can retain the facts you read, here
is a short article on the events leading up to the Battle of
Lexington. Pre-read it first. Then read the entire article as
rapidly as you can and time yourself before you take the
retention test at the end. Look for key words. Try to summarize the paragraphs as you go along. To give you a purpose,
we'll say that you are planning to write an article on the origins
of the American Revolution.

Starting Time   _____ **MINUTES** _____ **SECONDS**

Begin Timing:

"ALMOST everyone knows that the first blood of the American Revolution was shed at Lexington on April 19, 1775. Many believe that British troops cold-bloodedly fired on American militiamen who were simply exercising their right to bear arms in that chilly dawn. But who remembers now that the Boston Tea Party was the direct cause of the Lexington engagement?

"This celebrated incident — an overt rejection of the tax on tea — erupted on the rainy night of December 16, 1773. A well-disciplined collection of Boston's citizens — perhaps 125 in all and some rather fancifully disguised as Indians — boarded three British merchant ships in the harbor and tossed overboard £18,000 worth of tea sent out from England by the East India Company.

"When Parliament and George III heard of this defiance they demanded that Massachusetts Bay Province pay the full cost of the tea. The provincial legislature refused. Parliament then grimly passed an act to close the Port of Boston on June 1, 1774. It would remain closed till the tea was paid for. The King sent out Lt. General Thomas Gage as Military Governor of Massachusetts Bay, with four regiments of regulars to awe the Americans.

"For nearly a year Gage followed a policy of watchful waiting, hoping that the unrest would die down. But his spies kept him informed of the growing store of ammunition which the Americans were collecting in Concord, some 20 miles outside Boston. He knew also that "minute" companies were drilling on village greens from one end of the province to the other.

"His own military force was growing that winter. By the

spring of 1775 he had ten British regiments in Boston with a strength of more than 4,000 men. Gage realized that to send this army against the militia would cause armed rebellion. If he could just get possession of the ammunition it would serve the same purpose as a military victory. The provincial forces would be without means to resist.

"The course he decided on was a surprise night march to Concord. If all went well, his troops would seize the powder and be back in Boston by mid-morning — before the militia could be assembled. It seemed a sound enough plan, but from the start things went wrong. Even before the 700 grenadiers and light infantrymen embarked in boats to be ferried across the Back Bay to the point where they would begin their march, the secret was out. Paul Revere and William Dawes were on their way by different routes to alert the minutemen. After the regulars reached shore they were delayed for nearly two hours waiting for provisions to arrive. It was after one o'clock before they moved out.

"Alarm guns and ringing church bells soon gave gloomy evidence that the countryside was aroused. Excited messengers riding back from the direction of Concord told Colonel Smith, who commanded the regulars, that '500 armed men' were assembled in Lexington through which the road led. Smith sent Major John Pitcairn ahead with four light-infantry companies to reconnoiter.

"It was sunrise when Pitcairn came in sight of Lexington Green. Instead of 500 men, there were not more than 70 drawn up in two irregular ranks, with perhaps 40 onlookers. Pitcairn spurred his horse to the Green and demanded that the provincials lay down their arms. Captain John Parker, in command of the militia company, saw the futility of doing anything else. He ordered his men to disperse and not to fire.

"The British companies were now advancing in platoons

toward the militiamen. Some, but not all, of the Americans had obeyed Parker and were starting to leave the field. At this point, a single shot was fired, other random shots followed and then the first British platoon fired a volley. Two more volleys followed from the second and third platoons, pushing hard behind the first. When it was over, eight Lexington men lay dead; 10 more had been wounded. The only British casualty was Major Pitcairn's horse, but whether it was wounded by an American or a British bullet was not determined at the time — or later.

"Who fired the first shot? The Americans denied that it came from their side. Pitcairn swore he had given no order to fire, though he admitted that his regulars were nervous and had broken discipline in firing their volleys. To this day, no one knows who fired the shot that began a revolution. But of one thing there is no doubt. The road to Lexington began in Boston Harbor with the destruction of three shiploads of the East India Company's tea."

Stop Timing.

ENDING TIME _____ **MINUTES** _____ **SECONDS**

Timing Score. Length of selection, approximately 750 words.
Use the chart on page 8 or the equation given in Part One to figure your reading speed. Write it below:

TIMING SCORE _____ **WPM**

Retention Test

This article contained a good many important facts. The questions that follow will test your retention of the major points

1. What was the date of the Boston Tea Party?

2. How many men took part?

3. What was the value of the destroyed tea?

4. Who became Military Governor of Massachusetts Bay Province?

5. When was the Port of Boston closed?

6. Where were the Americans storing ammunition?

7. On what night did the British march out?

8. Who carried the alarm to the militia and the countryside?

9. About what time did the British reach Lexington?

10. How many American militiamen were assembled?

11. Who was their captain?

12. Who was the British major in command at Lexington?

13. How many Americans were killed?

14. Who fired the first shot at Lexington?

15. Why did the Boston Tea Party cause the Revolution?

If you made a good score on this retention test you have already acquired a sense of what you should retain in reading. Ten to 15 correct answers puts you in the superior class. If you did poorly, this test has provided a guide to the sort of facts you should look for next time.

CHAPTER TEN

Vocabulary — II

Most AUTHORITIES agree that the way to build a vocabulary systematically is to learn words in categories. This is how the experts work in those paperback books I mentioned in Chapter Six. The exercises are divided up according to groups of words centered in a single idea — the field of medicine, good and bad habits of people, words that grow out of various sciences, words about business and many more such categories. These books are efficient tools for increasing a vocabulary in a step-by-step manner — absorbing whole classes of words in the congenial atmosphere of related words.

There is only one way to master a new word. Look up its meaning in the dictionary (it may have several) and be sure to learn its spelling and its pronunciation. Then say the word aloud, for until you know its sound it will never become part of your active vocabulary. Better still, write a sentence that uses the word and read the sentence aloud. Then you will become familiar with the sound of the word in conversation. It will no longer seem strange to use it.

In looking up a word don't stop with the form you came across first. Learn them all — verb, noun, adjective, adverb — so you can use the word under any circumstances. Let's try one: "anthropology." Anyone who knows prefixes and suffixes can take this word apart instantly and see what it means. "Anthropo-" is a combining form for "man." The rest of the word, "-logy," is a suffix signifying the study or science of something. Therefore, "anthropology" has to be the study or science of man or mankind. Now what other forms of the word are there? A person who practices "anthropology" is an "anthropologist." The adjective is "anthropological." Adding "-ly" to the adjective makes the adverb, and there is no verb. Don't trip on "anthropoid," which doesn't refer to the science at all but simply means "resembling man." ("-oid" is a suffix meaning "like.")

Now for examples of sentences that might be made to fix these various forms in mind:

The science: "Through *anthropology* scientists have learned a great deal about the development of the world's races."

The scientist: "*Anthropologists* have made extensive studies of South Sea peoples still in a state of Stone Age culture."

The adjective: "An *anthropological* expedition spends many months in the field collecting data about individuals."

The adverb: "Working *anthropologically*, it has been determined that many European races migrated from the Middle East."

Manlike (the word that is not in this direct series): "The gorilla is the most powerful of the *anthropoid* apes."

Newspapers as Vocabulary Builders

Now consider how the newspaper can provide a special aid in adding words to a vocabulary. By using the newspaper's departments and columns a person will find words regularly in various categories so that he begins to build special vocabularies as the experts do.

Just what does that phrase, "special vocabulary," mean? Take sports. The baseball fan already has a specialized vocabulary. He knows and uses words and expressions which animate the sport. A man who knows nothing about baseball would be lost when the fan discusses the game with a fellow enthusiast. Every sport has special words and *idioms* peculiar to itself, and writers sometimes use them in a quite different setting to give color to their language. Their sense is instantly recognized if the original meaning is known. Just as an example, you might read in a light fiction story about a man who had tried hard to get ahead in business: "Jim had touched all the bases when he heard he was being considered for a vice presidency but he was left on third." This is just jargon to someone who doesn't know baseball (and I don't intend to explain it) but it is crystal clear to a baseball fan.

The gardener also has a specialized vocabulary — a big one — which would puzzle anyone who has never grown flowers and vegetables. In fact, the gardener would find it difficult to talk about his hobby to someone who didn't know the words because they are the natural way to express his thoughts and tell what he is doing. It is so much easier to say that he *mulches* his *hybrid teas* at the beginning of winter — something any gardener would understand — than to say he puts dead leaves around the plants of his garden roses to protect their roots.

So if a person follows sports and has a hobby he already possesses more than one specialized vocabulary. What will increase anyone's vocabulary in a dozen different directions is regular reading of the newspaper's departments and colum nists, particularly in the Sunday and weekend editions. Here is a list of subjects covered in this way:

books	food	music	sports
business	gardens	radio	television
education	health	records	theatres
fashions	homes	science	travel
finance	movies	society	weather

Some of these subjects will have no immediate interest for you, but try reading the most promising regularly. You will soon realize how many words have been fed into your vocabulary. Don't confine this "specializing" to the newspaper. Go to a well-stocked newsstand and look over the dozens of specialized magazines. They offer fascinating introductions to new fields of knowledge. Then, when your interest is captured, visit a book store and get a recent book on the subject. The world's knowledge, particularly in science, is increasing so rapidly these days that to keep up you must read widely. And all this enriches your vocabulary.

Specialized words constantly enter general reading, and they provide the key to advanced vocabulary building. Knowing their meanings and the way they are used contributes to smooth achievement in reading ease — and speed. It does more, for a wide vocabulary is basic to *comprehension*, the subject we take up in the next chapter.

CHAPTER ELEVEN

Comprehension

COMPREHENSION IS simply applying intelligence and pre
vious knowledge to any new piece of writing you decide to read
— and understanding it. Through the techniques of Modern
Reading, comprehension will be improved and deepened, since
these skills provide the means whereby the mind grasps ideas
more quickly. But the *quality* of comprehension will always
depend on what each individual brings to a new reading experi
ence from his background.

Each one of us has his own *comprehension quotient*. This
represents the sum of a man's knowledge, gained through pre
vious reading, through thought and discussion, through active
participation in various fields. For example, if you have read
one of Henry James' novels you are prepared for his somewhat
verbose and luxuriant style when you read another. You will
read the second novel more easily because you have *experience*
and *background*.

The person who has traveled widely in France and England
will read Dickens' "A Tale of Two Cities" — or any historical
novel or book of essays about those countries — with more
immediate *comprehension* because he is familiar with many of
the places mentioned. You can still understand the books

you have not traveled, of course, but you will *comprehend* less fully than the man with this experience. It is the same with any subject. You will always read with higher comprehension in a field about which you are already informed through reading or actual experience.

In Chapter Nine you read a brief article on the events leading up to the Battle of Lexington. You were asked 15 questions at the end to test your power of retention. All but the last tested only the ability to retain facts. The final question was also a test of *comprehension* — of how well you had followed the author's discussion. Your answer would reveal whether you had seen just how the Boston Tea Party set in motion a series of events which reached a climax 16 months later with the beginning of the War of Independence. You might have remembered all the facts required by the preceding questions. But if you did not answer the last one correctly you missed the point of the article.

So *comprehension* goes beyond *retention*, which is simply remembering facts and ideas. To comprehend fully you must not only get the *main facts* but see how the author marshals them to reach a certain conclusion. To do this, you must identify your stream of thought with his through *concentration*. Then all the pertinent knowledge which you have stored up in the past will be constantly feeding information that helps you to understand as you go along. Quite obviously the man who has read widely and experienced richly has an advantage in comprehending what he reads because he brings a broad background to each new reading adventure.

Reading Makes You Grow

Faster reading makes it possible for you to enjoy a thousand such adventures for every hundred you would have undertaken before. It has given wings to your mind. Now you have the means at your command to acquire the background of knowledge which is the only way to lay up the insurance of comprehension through a wide range of books and articles.

As to drills, you have already learned them, for the skills which underlie thorough comprehension grow out of the drills you have studied. To build comprehension your assignment is to *enrich yourself* in any field that strikes your fancy. Listen to fine music — and read about it. Look at great art and enjoy some of the handsome books which not only reproduce the masterpieces but tell you about the artists and their art. Delve into science and especially the rocketry and missilry which have made the space age a reality rather than a dream of the science-fiction writers. You will find many books, scrupulously correct in their science, which explain the conquest of space so the layman can understand it. They also expose him to the new words which technical breakthroughs have introduced into the language. Try popular books in some of the other sciences too — medicine, chemistry and biochemistry, biology, oceanography. Ours is an age of scientific discovery which is making historic advances in solving the riddles of life. Stretch your mind by reaching out toward new horizons. This is your opportunity to grow — and grow.

I have left great literature till the last, only because Part Three on "The Art of Reading" is designed to dwell on its pleasures. The new novels, the older ones you never had time to read, the modern histories, the social sciences — all these give perspective to your knowledge and taste in literature. For Part Three we have called in a group of experts to tell you how to get the most from your reading adventures.

Critical Reading

ALTHOUGH ONE DEFINITION of criticism is "to censure," its larger meaning is an evaluation, a judgment. A rave review of a new book which contains no word of censure is just as much criticism as a review without a kind word to say. In both cases the critic is offering his own judgment, and of course you may not go along with him either way. The critical reader does not blindly accept opinions. He reads them for their own interest and reserves judgment till he gets hold of the book himself.

In the previous chapter I talked about the *growth* which a person takes on when he becomes a better reader. One of the best examples of this is in *critical reading*. What you read has deeper meaning once you are evaluating and judging the content of all kinds of writing.

Nonfiction

The simplest kind of evaluation takes place with nonfiction — articles in which an author's opinions are up for judgment. You are reading partly for information here, because the author is marshaling evidence to support his conclusions. But his main purpose is to interpret the evidence according to his opinions. The reader will be judging whether he has made a good case and deciding to agree or to challenge parts of the argument.

Newspaper editorials are a good example of this kind of writing. The newspaper's editors take a position on a subject of local, national or world importance and justify it in a reasoned discussion. Columnists are frequently arguing a controversial point of view. Books and many articles in magazines set out to discuss causes or focus on conditions they feel need correcting.

There is no drill to learn in *critical reading*, but there should be two processes going on actively in your mind as you read. The first is to *ask questions*; the second is to *judge statements* the author makes in terms of whether all of them are readily acceptable.

1. Ask questions. You do not approach this kind of writing with the idea of finding fault. You simply read with questions in your mind. Probably you have always done that to some extent. With heightened reading skill and faster pace your mind absorbs ideas more quickly and is geared to take a more active part in evaluation. This adds a great deal to the stimulation of reading. There is nothing more challenging than matching intelligence and knowledge with an informed person, and this becomes the reader's purpose with critical reading.

Many of the questions that come to your mind will depend on the nature of the article itself. But there is a general pattern that can be followed with most articles. Let me illustrate with an example.

Suppose you are about to read an article titled "Your Money Goes Down the Drain." The subject is our government's aid program to underdeveloped nations. The title grows out of the author's discussion of what he claims to be a badly conceived and wasteful project for draining swamp lands in

Latin-American country. You know nothing about the situation under discussion. But there are some perfectly intelligent questions you can ask:

a. What is the author's *experience*? Did he *work* on this project, or *visit* the area?

b. What is the author's *background* — economist, agronomist, journalist, Congressional committeeman?

c. What seems to be his *purpose* in writing the article?

d. Does he appear to be an *objective observer*, or do you feel he is swayed by *prejudice*?

e. What sort of *evidence* does he offer? Does he present a series of *reports*? Or, on examination, is much of what he says simply his *opinion*?

Questions of this sort will govern the amount of skepticism which develops in your mind, and this will make your reading more interesting because your mind is actively engaged. Your questioning attitude will also alert you to distinguish between what is *first-hand report* and what is *opinion*.

2. Judge statements. The most believable statements in any article or book will be those which cite authorities or are made from personal observation. These are *reports*. When the author departs from documented reports he is presenting *opinion*. It may seem quite plausible opinion, but you should be reading to question whether the opinion seems justified in the light of known facts. Let me illustrate with a short paragraph about fishing:

"On the evidence of the authoritative book, 'North American Game Fishes,' the Gulf Stream off Florida's east coast is one of the world's finest sport fishing areas, with most of the notable large game fishes of the world. In a single afternoon I have seen sailfish, white and blue marlin, sleek tarpon and huge deadly sharks. No fish provides finer sport on a rod and reel than the blue marlin."

Of the three sentences in this paragraph, the first i *report*, since it cites an authority. The second is also a *report* since the author makes the observation out of his own ex perience. The third, however, is *opinion*, even though th author could probably have justified it on the basis of persona battles with various kinds of fish. You could not disput statements one and two. You might want to challenge th third. The author has offered no support for his opinion.

Broader Forms of Nonfiction

Up to now I have been speaking of articles and book designed to give information which is then interpreted by th author's opinions. A somewhat different kind of critical alert ness comes into play with nonfiction which has an importan literary quality — a fine biography or book of memoirs, essays a study of some period of history, philosophy and the othe humanities. You are no longer simply asking questions an judging statements. You are also judging *quality*. To do this a reader's *taste* in literature now becomes part of the critica equipment.

In a biography, for example, the author will be telling th facts about his man — bringing out the early influences on hi life from parents, boyhood friends and environment, showin how these played a part in shaping the course of his develop ment. The author will be both *interpreting the facts* and *usin his literary skills* in order to give you an estimate of the man an his times. The critical reader is now not only asking question

nd judging statements but forming his own estimate of the
author's literary performance.

He will consider the quality of the book's style and how
well the period has been re-created. And he will also be forming
his own opinion of whether the author's interpretation of
events is justified by the research which supports the conclusions. Some of this will be part of the text. Often it is
cited in footnotes, or in additional "Notes" to the chapters
usually placed at the end of the book. My advice is to ignore
these as you read, since they can be irritating interruptions of
of the narrative and often give no more than the source of an
anecdote. But this documentation should all be taken into
consideration when you are reaching a final evaluation. It is
the justification of the conclusions the author has drawn.

It is in this final evaluation that your own *taste* plays its
part, since judgment will be based on a comparison of the
book's *quality* with the quality of other biographies you have
read. This same element enters into evaluations of all kinds of
fine nonfiction which are read for self-enrichment. By the
breadth of his reading a person learns to evaluate the book he
has just finished and to give it a proper place in companion
literature.

Imaginative Literature

Another kind of critical reading comes into play with
imaginative literature — fiction, plays and poetry. The person
who has read fiction only for its entertainment quality will find
that critical reading introduces a rich new dimension to its
enjoyment. Without making a point of it, he becomes his own
reviewer, his own critic, judging a novel with an added gauge of
its beauty. He will weigh the novelist's latest book against his
earlier ones. He will consider style and the author's particular
genius for evoking mood in his scenes. He will be alert to how
well the author creates characters and keeps their actions

plausible. Instead of simply pushing on to find out "what happens," he will be thoroughly involved in a reading experience.

The same sort of critical apparatus is brought to bear in reading plays. The reader will appreciate the dramatist's skill in giving quickly a sense of the situation through the dialogue at the beginning of act one and then building his action toward the effect he intends to create. If you were watching the play the actors themselves would create much of this effect for you. Reading a play is a sharper test of the dramatist's ability. Now his lines must bring the stage and its characters to brilliant life in the reader's mind.

Reading poetry — and especially the more obscure passages of contemporary poetry — is an experience which many people say they never enjoy. But if you have not been reading verse lately, try it with your new reading skill alert. You may find that with your mind quickened to absorb ideas more easily what had seemed obscure and difficult before takes on new meaning and enjoyment.

These adventures in self-enrichment are the sophisticated reading experiences. They are part of the growth which I mentioned in the previous chapter. Now that the drudgery of reading is overcome you are freed to interpret as well as enjoy. These are the lasting rewards of *better reading*.

The Promise of Part Three

And now we are ready to consider the Art of Reading. Everything that was said in the two preceding sections is only prologue to the goal toward which we have been working — the real art of reading. You have now prepared yourself to move with confidence into the wonderful world of books.

It will be a rich experience with your newly developed skills, for books are an opening of new horizons, a road to new adventures, a source of unending pleasure and delight. People who have really learned to read are never at a loss, are never lonely. A good book is the best of friends, the same today and forever. But also, as Emerson has said, " 'Tis the good reader that makes the good book." This is why everything we have learned so far is of basic importance.

Let's see how far we have come at this point:

Part One explained the mechanics of *Faster Reading* and presented the drills and exercises by which speed can be achieved.

Part Two brought us through the more mature skills of *Better Reading* and stressed such important aspects of this development program as *Retention, Building an Advanced Vocabulary*, what *Comprehension* really requires and, finally, the rich rewards of *Critical Reading*.

Now the real adventure begins as we push along to the deeper pleasures of reading with the quickened skills and alertness which Modern Reading instills. The section which follows is devoted to the Art of Reading for pleasure and profit.

I have made a selection from a great variety of works that reflect wide differences in subject matter, viewpoint of the authors and literary style. The opening article, "In the Beginning Was the Word," tells about the importance of language in the development of human society. Like myself, I believe that you will be interested in this account of what man knows about the origin of his "most powerful tool in conveying his thought, in giving form to his activity, in formulating his hopes and plans for the future, and in preserving his memory of the useful past."

Next, Lewis Broad describes vividly how Winston Churchill led the British people in their defiance of the Nazi attacks on Britain in August and September, 1940.

Other selections are concerned with the strategy of the U. S. Navy in the Pacific during World War II; life and art in ancient Greece; the work of "Wild Bill" Donovan and his OSS; the life of Mohammed, the Prophet of Islam; how the earth looked to an American astronaut in space; what some modern philosophers believe about the future life; how Gary Cooper got his start in the movies; and who are the great writers in the English language in the twentieth century. The last passage, which is taken from Ivone Kirkpatrick's *Mussolini: A Study in Power*, relates the stormy—and pathetic— last hours of the Italian dictator.

Thus you will find in Part Three examples of historical and scientific writing, narration, description, philosophical discussion, analysis and biography—an excellent introduction to the joys of extensive reading!

I have often urged reading aloud for Modern Readers

since it is a wonderful way to sharpen perception and accustom yourself to pronouncing the unfamiliar words which are bound to crop up unexpectedly. Naturally you can't race along at the pace you use in rapid reading. Nevertheless, reading aloud can actually help you to absorb words quickly and build your vocabulary at the same time.

Reading aloud has a second big value too: It helps with phrase reading. Try this exercise: Look at your book only halfway through each line. Memorize the rest of the line while you read and glance up as you speak the remainder of the words. Then look down again and repeat the process. This will help your memory. But it also makes your performance more interesting to the members of your family who are listening because it keeps you in closer contact with them. Remember — this is a shared experience, a family get-together. You won't seem a warm part of it if you keep your eyes glued to the book.

In this connection, one charming and important aspect is the experience of reading to children and encouraging them, even before they can read by themselves, to memorize poems or brief narratives and recite them before the family and guests you have invited for dinner.

At this point, then, your instructor is saying good-by to you as you set out on an adventure that never ends. Your progress has brought you to the gateway of the wonderful world of books. Enjoy it!

PART THREE

The Art of Reading—
A Hawthorn Sampler

"In the Beginning Was the Word"

by Maurice Fabre

The following passage is taken from A History of Communications, Volume 9 in *The New Illustrated Library of Science and Invention. Mr. Fabre's work reviews the whole story of man's efforts to convey meaning to his fellow man through all the media.*

TO COMMUNICATE is to be alive, to be active, in relation with others. Helen Keller, deaf, dumb, and blind as an infant, lived at the lowest physical level until she was able to break through to the outer world. For communication is essentially an interchange, a question and a reply, an action and a reaction between an individual and the environment in which he lives. As everyone knows, communication in this sense is not confined to man but is shared to a certain extent with insects and animals. It may involve sight, touch, and hearing, gestures, expressions, and noises. But only man has developed that highly organized means of communication we call language, and his ability to use the spoken word to further his own purposes has had a lot to do with his dominant position on this globe.

"In the beginning was the word." Although man has always recognized and revered the power of language, other means of communication have been at his disposal—a gamut of gestures, a wide range of facial expressions, dances, and pictures designed to convey meanings in series; but since the beginning of human society language has been man's most powerful tool in conveying his thought, in giving form to his activity, in formulating his hopes and plans for the future, and in preserving his memory of the useful past. Language and society have grown up together; as the one grew more complex, so did the other. And no wonder, for they are different aspects of the same thing. Language is a form of social behavior, both expressing and at the same time giving shape to the beliefs and attitudes of people in groups—whether families, social classes, villages, tribes, or nations.

Considering the importance of language in the development of human society, it is astonishing to find how little is known about its origins. Writing, which by definition is a lasting record, occurred quite late in human history, but speech, which is by nature evanescent, may have arisen tens of thousands of years before writing first appeared. Who knows what language, if any, was spoken by paleolithic man—he whose bones, whose tools, whose paintings on the walls of caves have survived, but not his speech? The absence of any real evidence for the origin of human speech has opened the subject up to endless speculation. There were always those, of course, who held that speech was divinely revealed to man, a gift from God. Others, more logical but no less wide of the mark—including Democritus, Locke, Condillac, and Adam Smith—held that speech was adopted by mankind in convention; in other words, that it might be looked upon as an artificial creation legislated, so to speak, into existence.

From the nineteenth century onward, research into the origin of speech increased in quantity, seriousness, and intensity—but the results were as meager as ever. Among recent scholars several alternative theories have arisen and have been given colorful names which should not detract from their serious intent. There is, for instance, the "bow-wow" theory, which holds that human words first arose from imitations of natural sounds such as the barking of a dog. Or the "pooh-pooh" theory, that speech began with exclamations of fear, pain, pleasure, and the like, and its close relative, the "yo-he-ho" theory, that it started with grunts of physical exertion, or the "sing-song" theory, holding that primitive chants opened the way to speech. The Soviet scholar Marr considers that articulate speech began as an accompaniment to communication by gesture. And he bases all variations and combinations in subsequent speech on only four primitive sounds originally used with these gestures—sol, ber, yon, and rok. Other linguists believe that speech appears only when, as with children, a person's mental activity attains a certain level of development.

All of this admirable scholarship does little to clarify the actual origin of language. In fact, most of it is just as speculative as the persistent legend that the first and original language was the "language of the birds." This bizarre idea crops up among the ancient Egyptians, among the Incas of South America, and in the stories of Orpheus, Siegfried, and St. Francis of Assisi. It was quite seriously discussed by the medieval alchemist Fulcanelli, who wrote, "Those rare writers who have spoken of the 'language of the birds' accord it first place in the origins of speech. They say that it goes back to Adam, who used it to impose under God's will suitable names designed to define the characteristics of the people and things of creation."

The idea that there must have been *some* original language

is as persistent as the legend of the "language of the birds." Up to the end of the seventeenth century, Hebrew, the language of divine revelation, was held to be the original language of humanity. Leibnitz protested vigorously against this view, and gradually emphasis shifted from a search for the single original language to the fact, which was becoming increasingly obvious, that there were groups, or families, of languages. In attempting to unravel the relationships that linked the various tongues scholars began to develop a new tool for the study of the origin and diffusion of languages. Historical and comparative linguists, especially as applied to the problem of the Indo-European group of languages in the nineteenth century, began to provide a far sounder and more scientific basis for the study of language in general.

Years of careful and devoted scholarship have built up a picture of the world's languages, living and dead, which is almost frightening in its complexity. It is estimated that at the present time there are some 3,000 languages currently in use. In Europe alone scholars count 120. Then there are the dead languages, including Sumerian, Sanskrit, Avestan, Latin, Phoenician, Scythian, Iberian, and the rest. Altogether, it seems that almost 4,000 languages have disappeared during the course of human, and thus lingual, evolution. A strange example is the Etruscan, which can be read because it was written in a Greek script, but understood very little or not at all because its syntax differs from that of every known language.

And all these languages, living and dead—except for a few, such as the Baswue and the Japanese Ainu, which so far have defied classification—are complexly interrelated, through common origins, similar structure, word roots, and word sounds, thus falling into family groups, and subdivisions of these groups, some enormous, some quite insignificant. The largest overall groupings are the African, Semitic-Hamitic, Indo-European, Sino-Tibetan, Japanese-Korean, Ural-Altaic, Austronesian, North American Indian, and South American Indian. To these, many other groups and subgroups may be added ad infinitum: the Caucasian, the Dravidian, the Finno-Ugrian, 26 smaller families from North America, including Eskimo, Algonquin, Uto-Aztec and Iroquois, 20 from Central America including Mayan and Zapotecan, and 77 from South America and the West Indies, including Arawak, Carib, and Chibcha. The count for the Americas may not be very exact, for the classification of the numerous Indian languages is still in an embryonic state.

Of these so-called "families" of languages, some may be spoken by mere thousands of people, whereas the Sino-Tibetan languages of southeastern Asia are spoken by well over 600 million people, and the Indo-Iranian languages by some 400 million. Yet the latter is merely one subgroup of the great Indo-European, or Aryan, family of languages, which includes numerous other subgroups, such as the Germanic, Romance, Slavic, and lesser units like the Greek, Albanian, and Armenian.

The Indo-European family of languages, now used by about half of the world's population, is supposed to have stemmed from a small, compact area—variously located from the Iranian plateau through Central Europe to the Baltic— whose inhabitants migrated south and westwards before 2000 B.C., spreading the basic structure of their language to many diverse areas. Much later, Latin, a minor Indo-European dialect centered near the mouth of the Tiber River, spread by conquest over most of Europe and the Mediterranean. Offshoots of Latin and of the Germanic subgroup of the Indo-

European family—French, Spanish, and English—have now travelled around the world. Yet the close relationship of the many widespread branches of the Indo-European is nevertheless still quite clear. Travellers to Iran, for instance, are astonished to find that such basic words as "mother" and "father" are almost the same as in English.

Such a picture of languages and language groups growing and dying, evolving, splitting, competing, ever active and ever changing, seems utterly confusing until it is remembered that language is merely an expression of human society. Languages, like cultures, nations, civilizations, tend to disintegrate into local groupings unless there is a strong centralizing influence to enforce unity and growth. The Romans spread Latin around the known world, but when the Roman Empire broke up, Latin too, diverged into the various Romance languages we know today. Languages follow social, political, economic, and religious trends. Dying languages, for instance, have been revived for political reasons—as in Ireland and Israel. Even within a given language area, differences in dialect, usage, and vocabulary will reflect the fine shadings of class differences, of the differences between young and old, and between one profession and another. Language is indeed a form of social behavior.

It is for this reason that all attempts to create an artificial "universal" language have met with failure, despite the persistence of many inventors who seemed to have believed that language could be imposed on society, like laws. There is a record of a certain Arab, Sheik Mohyi-ed-Din, who invented a language called "bala balan." The enterprising John Wilkins, Bishop of Chester, published a grammar and dictionary of a language of his invention in 1668. Towards 1887 a Pole, Zamenhof, introduced the better-known Esperanto, of which

Ido is a refinement. In 1925 Occidental was created. Then came Interlingua and Gala, the latter formulated on the basis of the most recent of linguistic data.

All of these efforts merely illustrate the blindness of many scholars to the historical aspects of language. From earliest times language not only reflected the growth and change of human society in all its complexity, but played an even more positive role in shaping society and in building up that accretion of ways of doing things, beliefs, and knowledge we call human culture—or, in a higher manifestation, civilization. Before the invention of writing, and in the absence of written history, the accumulated lore, learning, and wisdom of the group was handed down from one generation to another by word of mouth. The spoken and remembered word *was* history. Without writing tools, speech had to serve; and without archives there was the retentive memory of certain men.

The oral tradition of prehistoric times remains a closed book to us. With the rise of civilization it was both supplanted and destroyed by literature, which etymologically means "written thing"—the narrator becoming a poet, or scribe. But in reading early epics, such as the *Iliad* and *Odyssey* (presumably written down by Homer about 800 B.C.), we are afforded at least a glimpse into that vast unwritten reservoir of tales, legends, myths, and heroic precepts which lay behind them and which were probably based upon Sumerian, Phoenician, or Egyptian originals. In fact all of antiquity reverberates with tales told and retold by anonymous voices. There were the Hebrew narrators, whose histories and exhortations were later incorporated in the Old Testament. There were Celtic bards, Anglo-Saxon scops, and Scandinavian scalds. Undoubtedly the last great keepers of the ancient oral tradition in Western civilization were the medieval German minnesingers, and the troubadours and trouveres of France who wandered from castle to castle singing of chivalry and love, the one in langue d'oc, the other in langue d'oïl.

An even closer imitation of how it must have been to live without the written word is furnished by the study of primitive peoples of more recent times. In innumerable tales, verses, fables, legends, and myths they give their answer to those three timeless questions asked by the painter, Paul Gauguin, at the top of one of his paintings: Where do we come from? What are we? Where are we going? But the remembered lore of the primitive is not confined to tales of the creation and of how to please the gods, but also aims to guide the hearer through the crises and requirements of daily life—birth, death, marriage, hunting, or the harvest.

Naturally, only a gifted specialist, a man trained in the intricacies of traditional lore, can be entrusted with the task of passing on such knowledge. In Polynesia, verbal transmission was carefully regulated and attained an astonishing degree of accuracy, and the itinerant professional reciters faced an audience that was in no sense passive, but participated and responded. Melanesians considered the word as of supreme importance, and identified not only the speaker but themselves with its importance, so that there were precise techniques not only for speaking but for preparing to speak. Genealogies, prayers, myths, poems, songs, and legends were the property of the reciters—the harepo of Tahiti, the tuhuna of the Marquesas Islands, the rogorogo of the Gambier Islands—who were trained by the priests and had to pass examinations, especially in the retentiveness of their memories, before they were allowed to instruct the next generation in the adventures of the great gods, Atea, Tane, Tu, Rongo, Oro, and Taaroa, the creator of the world.

Among the North American Indians, knowledge and transmission of the sacred texts was in the hands of the priests, or shamans. In common with other primitive societies, the Indians distinguished between myths, which were considered true, and tales, which were fantasies containing simple moral precepts for children to memorize. Myths, for instance, often told the story of the Great Ancestor—the coyote of the Columbia-Fraser plateau, the raven of the northwest Pacific coast, or the god Widapoki of the southwest. While Indian shamans were trained to impart these myths and tales by word of mouth, the shamans of the Eskimo, steeped in magic and fantasy, had as one of their chief functions the preservation and passing on of magic formulas used for a variety of purposes—to cure sickness, to ensure successful hunting, and so forth.

In Africa, too, the spoken word has been of central importance in preserving and handing down the myths and precepts of the many primitive cultures found there. Almost 250,000 different African tales have been counted by one specialist. Indeed, it has often been said that primitive Africa has a "spoken civilization." In this type of society one may still occasionally find a "master of speech" attached to a king or tribal chieftain. Traditionally, the "master of speech" was a kind of walking file with his head crammed full of information about his people and their relations with their neighbors, past and present. He acted as librarian, notary public, and historian all at once, and like the shaman or professional reciter often displayed incredible feats of memory. Such keepers of the oral tradition were of crucial importance to primitive society, but with writing and civilization their function has all but disappeared. And we are the losers.

Both primitive and prehistoric men were without writing;

but did they have any other means of transmitting ideas aside from speech? Certainly the rock paintings from the Neolithic period discovered recently in the Sahara region, as well as similar paintings by more recent primitives, seem to be close to "telling a story," which after all means communication.

And then there are the older paleolithic cave paintings from France and Spain which, taken as a whole, may also represent an effort to tell a story, as well as certain markings upon artifacts from the same era—possibly indicating ownership. Until the creation of writing, however, direct speech was the chief method of communication. But slowly man was groping his way towards new means which would enable him not only to set down that which he learned but to pass it along to others in a more accurate fashion.

Invaders Foiled:
August-September, 1940

by Lewis Broad

Mr. Broad's superb two-volume biography, Winston Churchill, *is distinguished by its quick-paced narrative style and brilliant characterization of the man.*

As JULY RAN out Churchill received the first warnings from the Continent. After the junketings, the German war machine began to stir. Hitler had given the order for the onslaught on Britain, an operation "bold and daring," as he termed it, in face of the "utterly determined islanders." It was to be completed, he ordered, by mid-September. His generals began to assemble troops, a quarter of a million of them, and his admirals the shipping. Both generals and admirals waited on Goering and the Luftwaffe to clear the skies. Unless the British planes were kept out, the admirals could not hope to shut out the British warships from the Channel, and if the British ships were there, then the generals knew it would be suicide to attempt the crossing—"pouring men into a sausage machine."

The Battle of Britain commenced. It ended as it started, in the air. Churchill followed its course with anxious attention. The kills-and-losses chart was his chief concern. Britain was heavily outnumbered and to lose plane for plane would put her out of the fight. Day after day the Germans flew over, bombing airfields and radar stations, the magic eyes of the defense. At night Churchill scrutinized the returns. Heavy toll was taken of the enemy but, gratifying as were the figures, they were not his main interest. What was the price the RAF had been made to pay? It was considerable, and as the losses mounted apprehension grew.

The front-line airfields bore the brunt of the attack. Some, like Manston and Lympne, in East Kent, were out of action until the damage could be repaired. Biggin Hill suffered severely. Churchill made visits to give encouragement to the men and sometimes to criticize. At Manston he complained of the delay in filling in bomb craters—it was feeble, far below the level of German performance.

In mid-August Churchill came to the microphone to report on the progress of the battle and to pay tribute to the young airmen in the words that register their fame—"The Few." Undaunted by odds, unwearied by constant challenge and mortal danger, the men of the RAF were turning the tide of war by their prowess and devotion. And then, the immortal phrase: "Never in the field of human conflict has so much been owed by so many to so few."

He gave words of praise to Beaverbrook for the astounding increase in the output and repair of machines achieved by an organization and drive "which looks like magic." But, magnificently as the Minister of Aircraft Production had labored, the handicap of years of neglect was not to be overcome in a couple of months. By sheer weight of numbers the Luftwaffe began to wear down the defense. Reserves of aircraft began to dwindle. The rate of loss was greater than factories and repair shops could replace and a shortage of trained pilots added to the anxieties of Dowding and the RAF Command. "The Few" were taxed to the uttermost limit.

As the fight went on, suspense mounted and anxiety grew. The attackers, regardless of their losses, pounded away at the airfields in southern England. Taking time off from Westminster, Churchill followed the engagements at close hand from air stations in Kent and Sussex. With everything at stake he had to be on the spot.

One afternoon in September he was present at Fighter Group headquarters, from which were controlled the squadrons in Kent, Essex, Sussex and Hampshire. In the operations room below ground he watched as battle was joined. Flashing bulbs marked the progress of operations. The Luftwaffe had fielded a full team that afternoon. The red lights soon showed that British fighters were up and after them. There were no more red signals to be flashed.

Churchill broke his silence. "What reserves have we left?" he asked.

"There are none," replied the Air Vice Marshal.

The defense had been stretched to the limit. The planes, their tanks empty, must begin to land to refuel. If more raiders came in they would catch Britain's pilots at a disadvantage. Happily, the Luftwaffe had been fully extended as well. The attacking planes flew off, save for the sixty that had paid the penalty.

There was relief in the operations room. Churchill had seen the turning point of the long contest. The Battle of Britain, though he did not know it at the time, had been won.

Goering, too, had been following the air battle with eager concern. He pronounced that the first phase had been won and that the RAF had been sufficiently weakened for raids on London to herald the invasion. His verdict was premature, his new directive providential for the defenders.

When the first bombs fell on London the Prime Minister ordered immediate retaliation to be made. The night following, 105 planes took off for a reprisal raid on Berlin. That week the German capital experienced the first attentions of British bombers, puny affairs by comparison with the havoc that was to come, but they had a decisive influence on the course of the Battle of Britain. Hitler, too, called for immediate retaliation and the rubbing out of British cities. London was the first target. Churchill's order to attack Berlin had been instrumental in diverting the Luftwaffe at the critical moment from the vulnerable target of the airfields. Londoners had to pay the price for the respite that gave the RAF the breathing space to recover. The RAF, as Goering was informed, might be down to its last reserves of Hurricanes and Spitfires, but sufficient strength remained to punish the vast target of bombers displayed by daylight on the route to London.

Meanwhile, on both sides of the Channel, the opposing forces stood ready. Over there, four thousand ships of the Nazi invasion fleet lay huddled in the ports from Rotterdam to Le Havre. Von Rundstedt waited on the Grand Admiral; the Grand Admiral waited on Goering. Hitler hesitated. The day was fixed—it was postponed. The RAF played havoc with the invasion fleet and, with the RAF so destructively active in the air, the Germans had no stomach for the Channel crossing.

Back in England the long alert continued. Watchers on cliffs and downs peered into the night. The scouts of the Navy, vigilantly patrolling in their little craft, were ready to signal the alarm before being blasted from the sea. In the West Country the code word was flashed—"Cromwell!" The church bells rang from their steeples. A Home Guardsman's vision of phantom parachutists had sounded the tocsin of alarm. Rumor improved on what imagination had begun. Bodies of German soldiers were washed ashore from the Channel. Europe heard the tale and smirked at the thought of a Nazi defeat, though, in fact, the troops for the invasion had not begun to embark.

The days were passing, the storms of autumn grew near and with them respite till the spring. Churchill could for a few months strike out from his calculations the possibility of imminent invasion. When the weather improved it had to be restored to the calendar of risk, so to continue an ever-present menace for many months to come, always to be guarded against. For there was no knowledge in Britain that Hitler had called off Operation "Sea Lion." It was not one for which the Fuehrer ever had a liking and he accepted the failure of the Luftwaffe in the summer of 1940 as decisive. Never again were the barges to be massed in the invasion ports. The victory "The Few" won in the air was the defeat, in its opening phase, of the invasion of Britain.

Churchill, in passing, could note that the new team for the direction of the war had successfully played themselves in. They were an effective instrument for the conduct of operations, and they gained in mutual confidence and understanding. But the swiftly rolling tide of battle gave little opportunity for applauding the score of vantage points. Without a pause, the Battle of Britain was merged into the long drawn-out ordeal of the Blitz.

To "The Few" the glory of the Battle of Britain; to the many the credit for endurance in the Blitz. The civilians were in the front line and they stuck it out through the black winter of the bombing. The Londoners proclaimed that they could take it and proved the words to be no empty boast. Take it they did—for fifty-seven consecutive nights—and so did others up and down the country as their turn came.

Churchill shared in all the perils of the bombings. He was heedless of danger, a source of anxiety for his Ministers and his family. When the bombs began to fall he would insist on having a look and was not to be induced into the shelters.

"Busybodies," he called them, as they voiced their alarm. "You can't teach an old dog new tricks."

He shared the hazards with his Ministers and with Members of Parliament. Plans had been made for an exodus from Whitehall if the pace became too hot. Ministers were to have been given a retreat in Warwickshire, and Parliament would have met in Shakespeare's town of Stratford-on-Avon.

All the arrangements were complete and pink passes were issued. Some there were who thought it time to move, but Churchill would have none of it—he was not going to allow any Hitler to drive him out.

"It's unthinkable that the Government should leave the capital," he said. "I, for one, will not go."

So they remained. Parliament sat in London throughout the war, despite everything that Hitler and his bombers could achieve. One move had, however, to be made.

Churchill's figure, dressed in a siren suit, became a familiar one after a raid. He would stand scowling at the wreckage of houses and offer words of sympathy to the homeless.

One morning he stood surveying the ruins of the House of Commons. An oil bomb had set the place in flames and a high explosive completed the destruction. As he looked on the rubble that had been the place of history and of his own parliamentary triumphs, the tears came. He made no attempt to hide them, but remained there mourning in sympathy with the Mother of Parliaments. The House had to find alternative accommodation, the peers obligingly placing the Upper Chamber at their disposal.

Downing Street suffered its damage. The kitchen of Number Ten was shattered by blast when Churchill was dining in an adjacent room. By a fortunate hunch, he had ordered the kitchen staff into safety only a few moments previously.

Had Churchill's view prevailed, the strident sirens that gave warning would have been silenced. "Banshee howlings" he called them, but not all were blessed with his fortitude under fire. The raid warnings had to be continued. He grew concerned over the interruption that was caused in the arms factories and the consequent fall in output. At his instigation a system of factory watchers was established, to give local warnings of danger overhead. In Government departments in Whitehall work fell behind during daylight raids till he put a check on the dugout routine. Departments, by his direction, were required to put in a daily return of dugout hours. Whitehall shelters thereafter were less frequented.

The Blitz posed its own pressing problems, each to be accepted as a challenge and to be met by the improvisation of the moment—incendiary bombs, the threat of famine, the menace to London's sewage. Nothing was too trivial to escape Churchill's attention, no problem too great for some solution to be contrived. Moved by his sympathy for the distress of the homeless, he took steps for the inception of the national scheme of insurance against bomb damage.

With the interest of a nonscientific mind, he followed the course of the battle of the laboratories. When the RAF navigated by the stars, the Nazi pilots flew by radio beam. Churchill introduced one member of the research team to the Cabinet, to give an exposition of the device by which the beam could be bent and the bombers diverted from their course, to drop their cargoes in the empty spaces of the countryside. Bending the beam could give little relief to London, a target not to be missed, but it contributed to the escape of some provincial towns with their vital factories.

From Midway
to Guadalcanal

by Fletcher Pratt and Hartley E. Howe

This chapter from The Compact History of the U. S. Navy *brings to life a crucial period of World War II.*

FOR SOME TIME there had been a violent dispute in the Japanese high command between the Naval General Staff, which favored maintenance of the perimeter of the sea empire, with extension only to the southeastward, and the fleet command of Admiral Yamamoto, who insisted the Empire would never be secure until the United States Fleet was destroyed. The specific step he proposed was the occupation of Midway Island. It was within long-range bombing distance of Hawaii, and once it was taken the Americans would surely be forced to commit whatever ships they had to an effort at recapture. This controversy was settled in typical Japanese fashion by sitting on both chairs. The Naval General Staff continued its preparations for a southeastward advance toward New Caledonia, Fiji, and Samoa, while Yamamoto drew his own plans. A determining factor was the Doolittle air raid on Tokyo; it was felt as an intolerable loss of face by everyone in the Japanese government, and though they did not know the raiders had come from a carrier they were quite sure that the seizure of the Midway outpost would prevent anything like that from happening again.

Events in the Coral Sea only reinforced this resolution. The view in Tokyo was that it had been a clear-cut Japanese victory; they were certain that both American carriers had been sunk, and there was bitter criticism of the admiral who ordered withdrawal. The plan for the Midway attack and occupation had already been laid on for early June, and it involved practically the whole combat force of the Japanese Navy—eleven battleships, their four biggest carriers, and heavy cruisers in the striking force, an invasion group to follow in transports, and a strong diversionary attack group to strike in the Aleutians and occupy their outer islands. Yamamoto's plan was to destroy the local Midway defenses by overwhelming air attack from the carriers and take over the island. When the American fleet came out to recover it, he would deliver a preliminary carrier attack, then go in with the big-gun battleships and finish matters.

It was a plan based on the assumption that the Americans would do what he thought they would do, and on ignorance of how much Pearl Harbor knew. Since before Coral Sea, American cryptographers had been reading Japanese cipher messages. At the date when Yamamoto's armada sortied from Japan, Admiral Nimitz had long been informed as to the exact composition of their forces and what they intended to accomplish. Enough of the Pearl Harbor battleships had been salvaged to work up a line of seven powerful, if slow, battleships. They put out of San Francisco in the latter days of May as line-backers in case the Japanese broke through, but Nimitz did not really expect to use them. He was going to base his defense of Midway on air forces. Army and Marine land-based planes were rushed to the island and long-range bombers made ready at Hawaii. The damaged *Yorktown* steamed fast north from Coral Sea, and a repair job that experts estimated as requiring ninety days was completed in forty-eight hours of hectic round-the-clock labor by yard workmen who were told this was a desperate emergency. *Enterprise* and *Hornet* were made ready for battle. Since Halsey had fallen ill, they were placed under command of the cruiser admiral Raymond A. Spruance.

It was one of the best choices ever made by Nimitz or anyone else. Spruance had no experience in carrier war, but he submitted everything to a process of cold, remorseless logic, and was known in the fleet as "the thinking machine." Yamamoto had thrown out a screen of scouting submarines to detect American movements from Hawaii. Before the scouts arrived Spruance had divined their coming and taken his carriers to sea in the area northeast of Midway, the spot least likely for the Japanese to find them. There he was presently joined by *Yorktown* with Fletcher, who was senior officer afloat and therefore in technical tactical command. Fletcher lacked an air staff, however, and left a good deal to the junior admiral.

This was the background. The great assault opened on June 3, when planes from two Japanese light carriers came through the mist and clouds that perpetually shroud the Aleutians to launch an attack on the American bases at Dutch Harbor. They found it much larger and better equipped than they had imagined. On the way back to their carriers the Japanese aircraft were suddenly set upon by Army pursuit planes, which had no business there at all, since by Japanese information there was no American airfield anywhere in the neighborhood. Harassed and perplexed, the Japanese admiral withdrew westward and settled for occupying the uninhabited islands of Kiska and Attu. His diversion had not diverted a single ship or plane from the American defense.

June 4 was a Thursday, with light winds and small clouds over the American carrier force, while the Japanese were well covered under a weather front. Nagumo, the Japanese carrier admiral, launched his strike against Midway early: one hundred eight planes, with the deck crews shouting the banzai as each one cleared. Half an hour later another one hundred eight followed. Radar warning sent every plane on Midway into the air—patrol planes back to Pearl Harbor out of trouble, a formation of Navy torpedo planes, one of Marine glide-bombers, and twenty Army planes going out to counter-attack; fighters up. The Japanese bombers burned out a fuel tank and a hangar, and their more numerous fighters got rid of most of the American defensive planes but, although they did considerable damage to the island, the Japanese flight leader radioed back that another strike would be necessary. The counter-attacking American planes were futile; the majority of them were shot down without producing a single hit on the Japanese ships, and Admiral Nagumo turned north under the cloud cover to refuel and rearm his planes.

At this moment there entered the combination a force of whose very existence the Japanese were ignorant—Spruance and the American carriers. *Yorktown* had flown the early morning search and when word came that the Japanese carriers had been located, Fletcher dropped back to take in his planes and sent Spruance on ahead with *Hornet* and *Enterprise.* The latter ran to within 175 miles of the Japanese position, and then launched full strikes—every plane on the deck of both the carriers—in the hope of catching the enemy planes that had taken part in the Midway attack while they were on their carrier decks, rearming. An hour and a half later, and that much nearer, the *Yorktown* also launched its planes, but only half a strike. The rest of its planes were held at that time, while searchers were flown for other carriers that were expected to be in the Japanese force.

Spruance's was one of the key command decisions of the war, but for some time it seemed that it might utterly miscarry. Nagumo's turn had taken the Japanese carriers well away from the positions where they were originally reported. The American planes had to hunt for them, and in the drifting banks and levels of cloud, fighters, dive-bombers, and torpedo planes became separated from each other. The result was that the torpedo planes, low over the water, reached the Japanese first and without fighter cover, receiving the undivided attention of the enemy combat air patrol. They were shot to pieces. Only four of them ever got back to the carriers; in *Hornet*'s Torpedo 8 squadron there was a single survivor, Ensign George Gay, who floated on a rubber seat cushion, settling himself just in time to see the most tremendous spectacle of the war.

For the four Japanese carriers had been forced into such radical maneuvers by the torpedo men that they could not get their planes away, and they were still on the decks, fueled and armed, when there came through the clouds the dive-bombers from *Enterprise* and *Yorktown*. The Japanese fighters were at the low levels where they had been killing off the torpedo planes; the dive-bombers had no opposition except anti-aircraft fire as they streamed down on the twisting carriers. Aboard *Enterprise* they could hear on the radio the fervid swearing of Squadron Leader McClusky as the first three bombs missed. Then the hits began—thousand-pound bombs from close in. Aboard three of the Japanese carriers vast sheets of flame leaped up to engulf everything; the gasoline tanks of the loaded planes burst, the torpedoes and bombs

129

they were carrying let go with the heat, the decks of the carriers folded back as though they were cardboard, streams of fire ran through their fueling systems and Ensign Gay on his seat cushion gazed with no little satisfaction at the long line of blazing giant ships, wracked by explosions. In five minutes the battle was decided.

But it was not yet over. One Japanese carrier, *Hiryu*, had slipped away north from the rest and was not hurt. About noon she began flying off strikes at *Yorktown*, which had lagged behind the other carriers and been seen by Japanese search planes. The strength of the American fighters was well down; at the cost of more than half their planes the Japanese got in on *Yorktown* and hit her with three bombs, one of which seriously damaged her engines. As a result when a torpedo attack came two hours later the Japanese got two crippling hits, and the carrier was under tow and helpless when a Japanese submarine sank her two days later.

In the meantime *Hiryu* had been located by American search planes and a powerful strike was flown against her from the two intact carriers. Her effort against *Yorktown* had nearly stripped her of planes, and she took the same treatment as the other Japanese carriers, bomb hits that stripped off nearly her whole flight deck and left her all afire inside. She sank at dawn; and in the meanwhile Admiral Yamamoto got the word that instead of a single American carrier being present, as he had at first assumed, there were three.

He made one more try. During the night, as the exhausted pilots aboard the American carriers drank coffee, discussed the events of the day and friends who were missing, then flopped into their bunks without even undressing, the Japanese fleet steamed eastward, trying to bring about a night surface action with the guns. But Spruance had also turned away east and toward morning the Japanese admiral realized that he would have no gunnery action, but instead would receive at dawn more attacks from those deadly dive-bombers, while American submarines were reported all around. He turned back to Japan, therefore, standing on the bridge of his flagship and brooding with staring eyes as he sipped rice gruel.

More Japanese died that day than on both sides in any naval battle of World War I. And as at Coral Sea it was not so much the total loss that counted, but where the loss fell. Four of the six Japanese carriers that led the attack on Pearl Harbor were gone, with practically all their air groups, planes, and pilots, the best in the Japanese Navy, which should have trained others. After the Battle of Midway, even Yamamoto was aware that he had lost the initiative.

The Shield of Achilles

An extract from The Glory That was Greece *by J. C. Stobart and R. J. Hopper. In this famous passage, the authors provide a rich picture of life in ancient Greece based on Homer's* Iliad. *The writing is leisurely and contains a number of unusual words.*

THE DESCRIPTION of the Shield in the eighteenth book of the Iliad is of twofold interest. It is a link with contemporary reality. It gives us a picture of Greek life which must be natural and universal, since neither dramatic nor religious motives interfere to distort it. The writer also is clearly describing a round shield with concentric zones of ornament, such as are found on Phoenician bowls of later date. The pictures are conceived as inlaid in various metals, gold, tin, silver, and "kyanos", or blue glass; in fact the poet is describing in every detail the technique of the wonderful inlaid daggers from Mycenae, although such weapons had ceased to be made for many hundreds of years. Here is the mixture of periods again. But obviously an idealising poet in describing such objects of art permits his imagination to excel anything that he has ever seen or heard of. Besides, it was wrought by the lame god Hephaestus, and the gods do not make armour such as you can buy at the shop.

First he made a shield great and mighty, decorating it in every part, and round it he threw a bright, threefold, gleaming rim, and a silver baldric therefrom. There were five folds of the shield, and on it he set many designs with skilful craftsmanship.

On it he wrought earth and sky and sea, and an unwearied sun and a waxing moon, and on it were all the signs wherewith heaven is crowned, the Pleiades and the Hyades and the might of Orion, and the Bear, which they surname the Wain, which revolves in the same place and watches Orion, and alone has no part in the baths of Ocean.

And on it he put two cities of mortal men, two fair cities. In one there were marriages and feasts. They were carrying the brides from their chambers through the city with gleaming torches, and loud rose the marriage-songs. The youths were dancing in a ring, and among them the flutes and lyres made their music. The women stood admiring, every one at her porch. But the men were gathered together in the marketplace. There a strife had arisen: two suitors were striving about the price of a man slain. One claimed to have paid in full, and he was appealing to the people, but the other refused to take anything. So both had hurried to have trial before an umpire. Crowds of backers stood around each to cheer them on, and there were the heralds, keeping the crowd in order. The old men sat upon polished stones in a holy circle with staves of loud-voiced heralds in their hands. With these they would arise in turn to give their judgments. There in the midst lay two talents of gold to give to the man who should speak the most rightous sentence of them all.

But round the other city two armies of warriors bright in mail were set. And there was a division of counsel among them whether to destroy it utterly or to divide up into two shares all the store that the lovely citadel contained. The be-sieged would not yet yield, but were arming in secret for an ambush. Their dear wives and innocent children stood upon the wall to guard it, and in their company were the men of age. So the warriors were marching out, and there were their leaders, Ares and Pallas Athene, golden both with golden rai-ment, both fair and tall, armed like gods, a conspicuous pair, for the hosts about them were smaller. But when they came to a place where they had decided to make the ambush, in a river-bed, where there was a watering-place for every beast, they sat down there wrapped in their shiny bronze. Then some way off two scouts of the army were posted to watch when they might see sheep and oxen with curling horns. And there were beasts moving along, with two herdsmen following that took their pleasure with panpipes, for they suspected no guile. But their enemy who had watched them leapt upon them, and swiftly cut off the herds of kine and fair fleeces of white sheep, and they slew the shepherds also. But the be-siegers, when they heard the din of battle rising among the kine, from their seats before the tribunes leapt upon high-stepping horses to pursue, and swiftly they approached. Tak-ing rank there by the banks of the river, they fought and smote one another with bronze-tipped spears, and Strife min-gled with them, and the din of battle uprose, and ruinous Fate was there taking one man freshly wounded and another without a wound and another already dead and dragging them away by the feet in the noise of battle, and her robe about her shoulders was dappled with the blood of men. They mingled like living men and fought and dragged away the bodies of their dead comrades.

Also he wrought thereon a soft fallow, a fat ploughland, a broad field of three ploughings. Many ploughmen were driv-

ing their teams up and down in it. And whenever they came
to the baulk of the field at the end of their turn a man came
forward with a cup of honey-sweet wine in his hands and
proffered it. So they kept wheeling among the ridges, anxious
to reach the baulk of the deep fallow, which grew dark behind
them, and, gold though it was, looked as if it had been
ploughed, so very wondrous was the craft.

There too he put a princely demesne, wherein hired labour-
ers were reaping with sharp sickles in their hands, some
swathes were falling thick and fast to earth along the furrow,
and the binders were tying others in bands. There stood the
three binders close at hand, and behind ran the gleaner-boys
carrying the corn in armfuls and busy in attendance. A king
with his sceptre stood in silence among them on the furrow
rejoicing in his heart. Some way off heralds were laying a
feast under an oak-tree. They had sacrificed a great ox and
were busy with it, while the women were sprinkling white
barley meal in plenty for the harvesters' supper.

On it also he wrought a vineyard heavy-laden with grapes,
beautifully wrought in gold. Upon it were the black bunches,
and the vineyard was set with silver poles throughout; round
it he drove a trench of kyanos and a wall of tin; a single
causeway led to it whereby the pickers walked when they
gathered in the vintage. Maids and youths were carrying the
honey-sweet fruit in woven baskets, and in the midst a boy
played a lovely tune on a high-pitched lyre, singing thereto
with his dainty voice the Linus-song, while the rest kept time
with stamping feet and leaping and song and shrieking.

On it he made a herd of straight-horned oxen. The cows
were fashioned of gold and tin; lowing they passed from the
midden to the pasture by a plashing river and by a shivering
reed-bed. Four cowherds of gold marched along with the

kine, and nine swift-footed dogs followed them. But among the foremost kine two dreadful lions were holding a deep-voiced bull. He was being dragged away bellowing loudly, but the dogs and the hinds were after him. The two lions had torn the hide of the great bull, and were greedily devouring the entrails and the dark blood, while the cowherds followed, vainly spurring on the swift hounds. But they, forsooth, instead of biting the lions, kept turning back; they would run up close to bark at them and then flee away.

On it the far-famed Cripple made a sheepfold in a fair valley, a big fold of white sheep, and steadings and huts and roofed huts and pens.

On it the far-famed Cripple fashioned a dancing-floor like that which Daedalus of old wrought in broad Cnossus for Ariadne of the lovely tresses. Therein youths and maidens costly to woo were dancing, holding one another by the wrist. The maids had fine linen veils, and the youths had well-woven tunics with faint gloss of oil. The maids had fair garlands on their heads, and the men had golden swords hanging from silver baldrics. Sometimes they would trip it lightly with cunning feet, as when a potter sits and tries the wheel that fits between his hands to see whether it will run. But sometimes they advanced in lines towards one another, and a great company stood round the lovely dance delighted, and among them a holy bard sang to his lyre, and among the dancers two tumblers led the measure, twirling in the midst.

And on it he put the great might of the River Ocean along the edge of the rim of the closely wrought shield.

So then when he had fashioned a great and mighty shield he fashioned also a breastplate brighter than the beam of fire, and he fashioned him a strong helmet, fitting the temples, richly dight, and on it put a crest, and he made him greaves of pliant tin.

I trust that the reader may be able to catch some glimpse of the picture even through the bald prose of translation. We are now in Europe for certain. It might be in Dorsetshire or Bavaria or Auvergne or Tuscany that these women come to their doors to watch the weddings go past, these honest ploughmen drain their beakers, and these weary harvesters look forward to the harvest supper. To this day you may see the peasants of Greece dancing in rings and lines, with agile acrobats to lead them, just as they danced on the shield of Achilles. History goes on its pompous way, leaving the peasant unaltered and the ways of country life unchanged.

The Secret War of the OSS

by Maria Wilhelm

Maria Wilhelm's The Fighting Irishman: The Story of "Wild Bill" Donovan, *from which this excerpt has been taken, is a good example of readable and popular writing.*

ONE OF THE OSS's earliest and finest achievements of which "Wild Bill" Donovan was especially proud was the famous invasion of North Africa by the "twelve apostles." Shortly after the COI was established back in 1941, a dozen foreign salesmen showed up in North Africa to peddle their wares, but under their nondescript, rumpled business clothes were such men as Harvard's famous anthropologist Carleton Coon and William Eddy, the president of Hobart College. As these unlikely salesmen went about their business, rather enjoying their new roles, what they were really doing was building up a formidable dossier of information on the locale and on the political situation as far as the French, as well as the Africans, were concerned.

They were also recruiting and training reliable local agents, with the net result that when General Eisenhower's forces landed in November, 1942, signal lights showed them the way, enemy guns on shore were quickly sabotaged, and the invading army was fully supplied in advance with a complete picture of all the German installations in the vicinity. The forces were also assured of the cooperation of French officers who had been ostensibly working for the Vichy Government. Speaking of the OSS in the European-African theatre (in the field the OSS was always subject to the Theatre Commander), Eisenhower declared: "In no previous war, and in no other theatre during this war, have resistance forces been so closely harnessed to the main military effort."

The stories of individual bravery are seemingly endless, and they could be told about a professor or a one-legged woman spy who parachuted behind enemy lines, or a bartender from the Yale Club in New York whose courage and language ability led him far from that safe haven.

There was the lone agent in Central China who spotted a Japanese cavalry force of ten thousand men and for eight long hours ground away at his hand-generator-powered, 31-pound transmitter, trying to arouse the Fourteenth Air Force in Chunking. Finally they got the message, and in a great mass bombing wiped out an estimated nine thousand of the cavalry troop.

An agent in France was traveling from Paris to Bordeaux, his only luggage a small suitcase containing his shortwave transmitter, the indispensable tool of a spy. While he waited for the train he was a bit uneasy that the station was so empty, but when the train pulled in he jumped on and settled himself in an empty compartment. Suddenly he heard a commotion outside and much barking of orders in German. The door of the compartment flew open and to his utter horror in marched the familiar figure of Field Marshal Rommel—the famous Rommel the Fox of the African campaign.

The agent hastily apologized for being so presumptuous as

to be on the same train as the Marshal, and roundly cursed the stupid ticket agent who had not told him this train had been reserved for German Army use. Bowing and scraping, he made for the door. But Rommel apparently felt big-hearted that day, and, remarking that after all civilians had to travel too, he motioned the unhappy agent back to his seat.

Afraid to disobey, he meekly sat down and breathed a sigh of relief as the Marshal and his adjutant left. A few moments later, however, the adjutant returned. The agent was sure that this time he had had it, but somehow he managed to look up casually and finally the adjutant spoke. The Marshal would like the gentleman's companionship for a cup of tea! The tea was duly drunk, but it was probably the least relaxing cup of tea in history!

Another agent actually managed to be accepted as one of Hitler's Storm Troopers, and one can only stretch one's imagination as far as it will go to try to guess what his existence must have been like. Still another, a German anti-Nazi, was a trusted officer of a large bank in Berlin. He had managed to hide his political beliefs, and even before the U.S. had come into the war he had contacted COI agents to tell them he was willing to work with them. He proved invaluable because he also trained two men in the Bank of France, and among them they were able for a long time to supply the OSS with the authentic currency of the moment which is such an indispensable part of an agent's equipment. To be caught with money that was not absolutely valid was one of the worst giveaways, and the Germans frequently called in various issues so that they could spot an agent who used out-dated money.

From the other side of the world came the story of the two Roman Catholic priests, Father MacAlindon and Father

Stuart. They had been missionaries among a remote Burmese tribe, the Kachins. When the Japanese invaded Burma in 1942, the priests were evacuated to India. They volunteered to go back into the Burmese jungle with an OSS team to set up contact with the Kachins, who disliked foreigners in general but who really hated the Japanese.

Father Stuart spoke Kachin, though with an Irish brogue, and they loved this striking figure with the Australian-style hat and a .45 revolver stuck in his belt. The good father was very like the general in the calm, absolutely fearless way he dealt with situations.

The story goes that he lost his temper only once, when a Kachin couldn't resist stealing his shiny, white false teeth one night. "Oh, Lord," Father Stuart prayed, "I know Thou sayest people must not take human life, but can't You please reclassify this one?"

The two priests worked tirelessly to interpret the strange language and even stranger customs of the Kachins, and, for that matter, to explain the Westerners to them too. The dangers were vivid because they were surrounded by Japanese, but the Kachins were marvelously cooperative. They had unusual mechanical aptitude and were born fighters. Whenever a battle was foreseen, the women happily cooked up a mess of monkey and deer meat in preparation for a victory feast. They persuaded the long-suffering OSS men to eat termites and one of their favorite stews, a concoction of little white bees cooked with assorted jungle herbs and vegetables.

They also taught them a thing or two about guerrilla warfare, including the use of two-foot bamboo slivers sharpened to a vicious point which they planted in the ground to pierce the feet of unwary Japanese. (This device has shown up in Vietnam and to cope with it the U.S. Army has developed a new kind of shoe with a steel mesh sole.)

Besides harassing the Japs and doing much damage to their installations, this Kachin-OSS team saved hundreds of Allied fliers downed in the jungle. So effective were they that they accounted for over five thousand dead Japanese, with a loss of only fifteen Americans and seventy Kachins.

These are only a few of the hundreds of exploits carried out by Donovan's men and women. Nor, as one can imagine, was the general one to run his show from a safe desk in Washington. There rarely was an Allied landing without Bill in the lead boat, and it became a joke in Washington that if Bill's car remained parked all day in front of his Georgetown house it was a sure bet there would be a new offensive soon.

Mohammed and Islam

by Francesco Gabrieli

This passage from The Arabs: A Compact History *by Francesco Gabrieli supplies a brief profile of the great religious leader.*
For the wordophiles, a short word game follows the selection.

The only certain source relating to the life of Mohammed is the Koran itself, followed immediately by the canonical biography (*Sira*) as it was formed in the beginnings of the second century of Islam. It found its classic expression in the *Life of the Prophet* by Ibn Ishàq (died ca. 767), which has come down to us in a somewhat reduced and annotated edition by Ibn Hishàm (died 834), and in extracts from the most ancient chroniclers like Tàbari (died 923). Other important sources are the "Book of Military Expeditions" (*Maghazi*) of the Prophet by al-Wàqidi (died 822), and the great biographical collection on his Companions (*Tabaqàt as-sahaba*) by Ibn Saad (died 899). In modern times radical criticism has inclined, perhaps excessively, to invalidate the historical worth of all these sources, judging them to be *hagiographical* combinations and deformations. A more tempered critical examination must always make use of them with vigilant caution and recognize, especially for the more remote period of Mohammed's life, that we know very little outside of that which is drawn directly from the Koran.

Strictly speaking, we do not know the very year of the Prophet's birth: the *synchronism* with the "Year of the Elephant," i.e., 570, can be accepted in an approximate way; indeed some scholars have sought to reduce it almost by a decade. Doubt has also been expressed, wrongly we think, regarding the name Mohammed itself (which *etymologically* means "the much praised one"), a name not unknown in pre-Moslem times. What is certain is his origin in the Quraysh clan of the Banu Hashim. Mohammed was the pothumous son of the merchant Abdallàh, esteemed but not rich, who died during a journey far from his native country, and of Aminah, who herself left the child an orphan when he was barely six years old. The boy grew up first under the care of his paternal grandfather Abd al-Mùttalib. Later he was entrusted to an uncle Abu Talib, father of that Ali who was to become one of his most faithful first companions, then his son-in-law and finally his fourth successor as Caliph. What is certain among the facts of the youthful life of Mohammed prior to his vocation, the broad purposes of which were effected between his thirtieth and fortieth year, are his marriage to the rich widow Khadijah, for whom he had also traveled and traded, and his contacts with Christian elements of the desert and, perhaps, of Syria, and with Hanifs. They have been embellished by tradition but contain a historical core of a highly probable character. All the varied elements of the religious life of Arabia, as we have outlined above—urban and Bedouin paganism, Christianity and initially Judaism to a minor degree, vague conceptions and *monotheistic* aspirations—found acceptance, elaboration, and a reaction in the receptive spirit of this man. We know little about his crisis which erupted around 610, in the visions and in the "voices" of his holy retreat on Mount Hirà.

Of the two types of inspiration which tradition has bequeathed to us, the visual and the oral, it is quite difficult to determine which may have been the first and the one that prevailed in the initial phase. Later, he named the angel Gabriel as the celestial creature who appeared to him and, with irresistible force, imposed the monotheistic assertion contained in the most ancient koranic *versicles*; the same creature was considered as the normal means for transmitting the subsequent revelations. The fundamental concepts of this monotheistic assertion, in the first phase, were the repudiation of the native *polytheism,* in order to exalt the only Allah above and against every other divinity (some casual attempts at a compromise were quickly withdrawn and overcome), the imminent judgment with the inescapable final retribution of good and evil, praise of God the Creator and of His marvels, and the certain resurrection beyond the grave. All the more ancient koranic *suras* play upon these themes over and over again, and they reflect at one and the same time the nascent *polemics,* and the struggle with a hostile *ambience.* In fact, the new preachment offended the native traditions and piety, sincerely felt in at least some Meccan circles. At the same time it also irked the elementary rationalism which found the concept of life after death repugnant, as well as the material, economic interests of that mercantilistic *oligarchy* which was naturally conservative. The notion that Mohammed's message was primarily social in character and aim, is a fantasy of the *positivistic* and Marxist *historiography* and its current *obdurate* practitioners. What is true, rather, is that the new theological and *eschatological* conception, like primitive Christianity, nourished itself on the discontent over the injustice of which the earth is full, and with its supra-mundane hopes it preferably attracted to itself those who had suffered most from this injustice. Mohammed's first followers were recruited above all among the humble, petty artisans and merchants, buyers, slaves—not without the cooperation of that which we shall call the Meccan middle class. But from the ruling class, from the Quraysh aristocracy came a resolute and gradually ever increasing rigid opposition. Then and later the Prophet, to be sure, tried to gain the latter to his cause with approaches that were hardly in keeping with an *intransigent* social reformer, but only the clear indication of his triumph, which occurred very much later, succeeded in disarming the aristocracy of its resistance. In those first years the resistance was dogged, although bloodless, consisting essentially of vexations, repulses and mockery, which at one time culminated in an attempt to place the innovator and his small community beyond the pale. The boycott was broken through the intervention of authoritative members of his own clan in which, though they were pagans, the inherited law of the solidarity of blood still spoke loudly: but the situation in Mecca at one moment seemed so untenable that it induced part of the small community to migrate beyond the Red Sea, to Ethiopia facing Arabia. The more or less authentic speech which tradition places in the mouth of those refugees in the presence of the Negus aptly summarizes, albeit with some polemical exaggeration, the import of the more ancient preachment of Mohammed: "O king, we were a barbarous people of idolaters, who committed shameful misdeeds, despised the ties of blood, violated the obligations of hospitality: a people among whom the stronger devoured the weaker. Such were we until God sent us an apostle from our very bosom, whose descent, veracity and continence are known to us: and

146

he called us to God, to recognize Him alone and to worship Him, repudiating the stones and the idols which we and our forefathers worshipped in His stead. He has ordered us to be truthful, to render loyally the deposit confided to us, to respect the ties of blood and of hospitable protection, to abstain from illicit acts and from shedding blood; he has forbidden us to indulge in any *turpitude* and deceit, to devour the goods of the orphan and to calumnify honest women, he has commanded us to worship God, and to place nothing beside Him, to observe canonical prayer, the legal alms, the fast. We have believed in him, we have followed him in the precepts which he has brought to us from God; hence our people have become hostile to us, and have persecuted us . . ."

In comparison with many other methods of persecution, suffered and later even practiced by a new faith on the march, those employed by the Quraysh towards young Islam may seem mild enough: this does not remove the fact that the Prophet certainly lived through many bitter and anxiety-ridden hours during that vigil. It dragged on for about a decade and terminated, as is known, with the decisive act of his career; he abandoned the city of his birth with all his followers in order to establish himself and his community in Medina. This "hegira" of September 622 marks the beginning of a new era not only in the Moslem calendar, but in the personal history of Mohammed, and in that of Arabia and of Islam.

A Vocabulary Game

1. **hagiographical**
2. **synchronism**
3. **etymological**
4. **monotheistic**
5. **polytheism**
6. **versicles**
7. **polemics**
8. **ambience**
9. **oligarchy**
10. **positivistic**

a. above earthly things
b. pertaining to death, resurrection and immortality
c. hardened against moral or mollifying influences
d. pertaining to sacred writings
e. concurrence in time of two or more events
f. surrounding
g. pertaining to theory that natural phenomena are the only knowable things
h. refusing to compromise
i. the writing of history
j. government by the few

11. **historiography** k. short verse said by a priest followed by response from the people

12. **obdurate** l. pertaining to doctrine or belief that there is one God

13. **eschatological** m. pertaining to origin and derivation of words

14. **supra-mundane** n. the doctrine or belief in a plurality of gods

15. **intransigent** o. inherent baseness of principles

16. **turpitude** p. art or practice of disputation or controversy

---

1. D	5. N	9. J	13. B
2. E	6. K	10. G	14. A
3. M	7. P	11. I	15. H
4. L	8. F	12. C	16. O

The Earth from Space

by John Glenn

The Space Age—like the Age of Discovery—introduces man to new challenges, dangers, and opportunities. One of America's space pioneers reports his observations in this excerpt from More Great True Adventures *selected by Lowell Thomas and Lowell Thomas, Jr.*

WEIGHTLESSNESS was a pleasant experience. I reported I felt fine as soon as the spacecraft separated from the launch vehicle, and throughout the flight this feeling continued to be the same.

Approximately every 30 minutes throughout the flight I went through a series of exercises to determine whether weightlessness was affecting me in any way. To see if head movement in a zero g environment produced any symptoms of nausea or vertigo, I tried first moving, then shaking my head from side to side, up and down, and tilting it from shoulder to shoulder. In other words, moving my head in roll, pitch, and yaw. I began slowly, but as the flight progressed, I moved my head more rapidly and vigorously until at the end of the flight I was moving as rapidly as my pressure suit would allow.

In another test, using only eye motions, I tracked a rapidly moving spot of light generated by my finger-tip lights. I had no problem watching the spot and once again no sensations of dizziness or nausea. A small eye chart was included on the instrument panel, with letters of varying size and with a "spoked wheel" pattern to check both general vision and any tendency toward astigmatism. No change from normal was apparent.

An "oculogyric test" was made in which turning rates of the spacecraft were correlated with sensations and eye movements. Results were normal. Preflight experience in this test and a calibration had been made at the Naval School of Aviation Medicine, Pensacola, Fla., with Dr. Ashton Graybiel, so that I was thoroughly familiar with my reactions to these same movements at 1 g.

To provide medical data on the cardiovascular system, at intervals, I did an exercise which consisted of pulling on a bungee cord once a second for 30 seconds. This exercise provided a known workload to compare with previous similar tests made on the ground. The flight surgeons have reported the effect that this had on my pulse and blood pressure. The effect that it had on me during the flight was the same effect that it had on the ground—it made me tired.

Another experiment related to the possible medical effects of weightlessness was eating in orbit. On the relatively short flight of Friendship 7, eating was not a necessity, but rather an attempt to determine whether there would be any problem in consuming and digesting food in a weightless state. At no time did I have any difficulty eating. I believe that any type of food can be eaten as long as it does not come apart easily or make crumbs. Prior to the flight, we joked about taking along some normal food such as a ham sandwich. I think this would be practical and should be tried.

Sitting in the spacecraft under zero g is more pleasant than under 1 g on the ground, since you are not subject to any pressure points. I felt that I adapted very rapidly to weightlessness. I had no tendency to overreach nor did I experience any other sign of lack of coordination, even on the first movements after separation. I found myself unconsciously taking advantage of the weightless condition, as when I would leave a camera or some other object floating in space while I attended to other matters. This was not done as a preplanned maneuver but as a spur-of-the-moment thing when another system needed my attention. I thought later about how I had done this as naturally as if I were laying the camera on a table in a 1 g field. It pointedly illustrates how rapidly adaptable the human is, even to something as foreign as weightlessness.

We discovered from this flight that some problems are still to be solved in properly determining how to stow and secure equipment that is used in a space vehicle. I had brought along a number of instruments, such as cameras, binoculars, and a photometer, with which to make observations from the spacecraft. All of these were stowed in a ditty bag by my right arm. Each piece of equipment had a 3-foot piece of line attached to it. By the time I had started using items of the equipment, these lines became tangled. Although these lines got in the way, it was still important to have some way of securing the equipment, as I found out when I attempted to change film. The small canisters of film were not tied to the ditty bag by lines. I left one floating in midair while working with the camera, and when I reached for it, I accidentally hit it and it floated out of sight behind the instrument panel.

As I looked back at the earth from space, colors and light intensities were much the same as I had observed when flying at high altitude in an airplane. The colors observed when looking down at the ground appeared similar to those seen from 50,000 feet. When looking toward the horizon, however, the view is completely different, for then the blackness of space contrasts vividly with the brightness of the earth. The horizon itself is a brilliant, brilliant blue and white.

It was surprising how much of the earth's surface was covered by clouds. The clouds can be seen very clearly on the daylight side. The different types of clouds—vertical developments, stratus clouds, and cumulus clouds—are readily distinguished. There is little problem identifying them or in seeing the weather patterns. You can estimate the relative heights of the cloud layers from your knowledge of the types or from the shadows the high clouds cast on those lower down. These observations are representative of information which the scientists of the U.S. Weather Bureau Meteorological Satellite Laboratory had asked Project Mercury to determine. They are interested in improving the optical equipment in their Tiros and Nimbus satellites and would like to know if they could determine the altitude of cloud layers with better optical resolution. From my flight I would say it is quite possible to determine cloud heights from this orbital altitude.

Only a few land areas were visible during the flight because of the cloud cover. Clouds were over much of the Atlantic, but the western (Sahara Desert) part of Africa was clear. In this desert region I could plainly see dust storms. By the time I got to the east coast of Africa where I might have been able to see towns, the land was covered by clouds. The Indian Ocean was the same.

Western Australia was clear, but the eastern half was overcast. Most of the area across Mexico and nearly to New Orleans was covered with high cirrus clouds. As I came across the United States I could see New Orleans, Charleston, and Savannah very clearly. I could also see rivers and lakes. I think the best view I had of any land area during the flight was the clear desert region around El Paso on the second pass across the United States. I could see the colors of the desert and the irrigated area north of El Paso. As I passed off the east coast of the United States I could see across Florida and far back along the Gulf Coast.

Over the Atlantic I saw what I assume was the Gulf Stream. The different colors of the water are clearly visible.

I also observed what was probably the wake of a ship. As I was passing over the recovery area at the end of the second orbit, I looked down at the water and saw a little "V". I checked the map. I was over recovery area G at the time, so I think it was probably the wake from a recovery ship. When I looked again, the little "V" was under a cloud. The change in light reflections caused by the wake of a ship are sometimes visible for long distances from an airplane and will linger for miles behind a ship. This wake was probably what was visible.

I believe, however, that most people have an erroneous conception that from orbital altitude, little detail can be seen. In clear desert air, it is common to see a mountain range 100 or so miles away very clearly, and all that vision is through atmosphere. From orbital altitude, atmospheric light attenuation is only through approximately 100,000 feet of atmosphere, so it is even more clear. An interesting experiment for future flights can be to determine visibility of objects of different sizes, colors, and shapes.

Obviously, on the night side of the earth, much less was visible. This may have been due not only to the reduced light, but also partly to the fact that I was never fully dark adapted. In the bright light of the full moon, the clouds are visible. I could see vertical development at night. Most of the cloudy areas, however, appeared to be stratoform.

The lights of the City of Perth, in western Australia, were on and I could see them well. The view was similar to that seen when flying at high altitude at night over a small town. South of Perth there was a small group of lights, but they were much brighter in intensity. Inland there was a series of four or five towns lying in a line running from east to west. Knowing that Perth was on the coast, I was just barely able to see the coastline of Australia. Clouds covered the area of eastern Australia around Woomera, and I saw nothing but clouds from there across the Pacific until I was east of Hawaii. There appeared to be almost solid cloud cover all the way.

Just off the east coast of Africa were two large storm areas. Weather Bureau scientists had wondered whether lightning could be seen on the night side, and it certainly can. A large storm was visible just north of my track over the Indian Ocean and a smaller one to the south. Lightning could be seen flashing back and forth between the clouds but most prominent were lightning flashes within thunderheads illuminating them like light bulbs.

Some of the most spectacular sights during the flight were sunsets. The sunsets always occurred slightly to my left, and I turned the spacecraft to get a better view. The sunlight coming in the window was very brilliant, with an intense clear white light that reminded me of the arc lights while the spacecraft was on the launching pad.

I watched the first sunset through the photometer, which had a polarizing filter on the front so that the intensity of the sun could be reduced to a comfortable level for viewing. Later I found that by squinting, I could look directly at the sun with no ill effects, just as I can from the surface of the earth. This accomplished little of value but does give an idea of intensity.

The sun is perfectly round as it approaches the horizon. It retains most of its symmetry until just the last sliver is visible. The horizon on each side of the sun is extremely bright, and when the sun has gone down to the level of this bright band of the horizon, it seems to spread out to each side of the point where it is setting. With the camera I caught the flattening of the sun just before it set. This is a phenomenon of some interest to the astronomers.

As the sun moves toward the horizon, a black shadow of darkness moves across the earth until the whole surface, except for the bright band at the horizon, is dark. This band is extremely bright just as the sun sets, but as time passes the bottom layer becomes a bright orange and fades into reds, than on into the darker colors, and finally off into the blues and blacks. One thing that surprised me was the distance the light extends on the horizon on each side of the point of the sunset. I think that the eye can see a little more of the sunset color band that the camera captures. One point of interest was the length of time during which the orbital twilight persisted. Light was visible along the horizon for 4 to 5 minutes after the sunset, a long time when you consider that sunset occurred 18 times faster than normal.

The period immediately following sunset was of special interest to the astronomers. Because of the atmospheric light scattering, it is not possible to study the region close to the sun except at the time of a solar eclipse. It had been hoped that from above the atmosphere the area close to the sun could be observed. However, this would require a period of dark adaptation prior to sunset. An eye patch had been developed for this purpose, which was to be held in place by special tape. This patch was expected to permit one eye to be night adapted prior to sunset. Unfortunately, the tape proved unsatisfactory and I could not use the eye patch. Observations of the sun's corona and zodiacal light must await future flights when the pilot may have an opportunity to get more fully dark adapted prior to sunset.

Another experiment suggested by our advisors in astronomy was to obtain ultraviolet spectrographs of the stars in the belt and sword of Orion. The ozone layer of the earth's atmosphere will not pass ultraviolet light below 3,000 angstroms. The spacecraft window will pass light down to 2,000 angstroms. It is possible, therefore, to get pictures of the stars from the Mercury spacecraft which cannot be duplicated by the largest telescopes on the ground. Several ultraviolet spectrographs were taken of the stars in the belt of Orion. They are being studied at the present time to see whether useful information was obtained.

The biggest surprise of the flight occurred at dawn. Coming out of the night on the first orbit, at the first glint of sunlight on the spacecraft, I was looking inside the spacecraft checking instruments for perhaps 15 to 20 seconds. When I glanced back through the window my initial reaction was that the spacecraft had tumbled and that I could see nothing but stars through the window. I realized, however, that I was still in the normal attitude. The spacecraft was surrounded by luminous particles.

These particles were a light yellowish green color. It was as if the spacecraft were moving through a field of fireflies. They were about the brightness of a first magnitude star and appeared to vary in size from a pinhead up to possibly ⅜ inch. They were about 8 to 10 feet apart and evenly distributed through the space around the spacecraft. Occasionally, one or two of them would move slowly up around the spacecraft and across the window, drifting very, very slowly, and would then gradually move off, back in the direction I was looking. I observed these luminous objects for approximately 4 minutes each time the sun came up.

Existentialism

by Maurice and Louis Becqué

Maurice and Louis Becqué combine philosophy and religion in this brief essay from their work, Life After Death, *volume 28 in* The Twentieth Century Encyclopedia of Catholicism.

THE "ANGUISH" (*angoisse*) revealed by contemporary literature, whether "committed" or not, has become an object of study for philosophy, since it, too, studies the impulsions of the soul. In fact the philosophies of our day have abandoned the serene regions of objectivity, essence and the universal for subjectivity, existence and the particular. Never before, perhaps, have philosophy and literature been so closely linked. These manifestations of modern thought deserve our attention because of their attitude to the future life.

In general, we can say that all these philosophies are more or less "existentialist." The upheaval of two great wars, the anxiety and insecurity arising from the overthrow of firmly established régimes and systems, have not been without influence on their development. Yet long before the shock of the first world war the Danish philosopher, Søren Kierkegaard, in *Fear and Trembling,* had analysed the tragic element of existence. The aesthetic attitude of abandonment to the present moment is untenable. Life is only made bearable by transcending the aesthetic and even the ethical sphere, to arrive by faith at the religious plane. This faith is truth, but "truth for me," and therefore pure subjectivity. Every truth is subjectivity. Man will be what he will be, according to the idea he forms of his being. His eternity is decided and planned in time. He will find God, who became incarnate to save him, by setting himself up as "I" before himself. The absurdity, the obscurity of the individual life, ineffable as is every individual thing, are experienced by the believer. But he commits himself only with fear and trembling, for he can never be sure of being chosen by the Lord.

Subjectivity is sister to phenomenology. The famous professor Husserl (†1938), father of this new philosophy, seems to have been prepared to consider as "objects" only those to which consciousness applies. He confined his description to that which appears (the phenomenon) and remains identical, not concerning himself with essence or even existence. A thing is "put there" (*ob-ject*): it alone has a content which can be described to the subject, a content which consciousness applies. By limiting the perception of consciousness, Husserl gave a certain importance to the subjective and prepared the way for our modern existentialists.

Martin Heidegger continues Husserl's descriptive method but, in contrast to his master, applies it to existence itself. The only being on earth which is capable of conceiving that it exists is man. Human existence means being there, outside, along with things (*ex-istere*). It is, he says, "being-in-the-world," the *Dasein.* Death belongs to the structure of "being-in-the-world." It constitutes the last, supreme existential possibility. Because man is thrust into the world, he submits to its division. He reaches out to the past, the present and the future and is aware of historicity. Above all he looks to the future. By this aspiration towards what is to come he rises above himself. But what is to come is death, looming on the horizon: so far from passing through death to a fullness of being, he finds only nothingness before him.

Less of a pessimist, more religious, nearer to Kierkegaard, comes Jaspers. His position is that every existing thing thinks of itself, feels itself and determines its being. It at once encounters obstacles, situations such as space, time, pain and guilt, which limit the tendency to transcendence. But Jaspers ascribes a high value to these obstacles. They prove that man can neither be self-sufficient nor find an end in himself, in his own existence. This existence reveals a relation with God, with his mysterious presence. By a free choice the human creature can attain to the eternal and absolute Being. The divine greatness, transcendence, is merged with what philosophers call immanence, that is, the fact of being within. Thus appears the "inwardness" of the living God, who is my own, to whom in the hour of anguish I can offer or refuse myself. In Jaspers' meaning, human existence, more vertical than with the gloomy Heidegger, has the power to rise from failure to failure, up to him who transcends all. Through this final step, its drama culminates, at the fall of the curtain, in the encounter with the unique Other.

The existential philosophies, then, are not unanimous in refusing the appeal from this present world to the divine "beyond."

In France, especially since the last war, a whole body of literature has sprung up in which the ideas called existentialist have been popularized. The leader of these thinkers in the line of Heidegger is Jean-Paul Sartre. More of a psychologist, perhaps, than a metaphysician, he has described with a master hand the *taedium vitae,* the incurable ennui in which human existence is plunged. Man is a being who is in process of becoming. He is nothing more, being "condemned to liberty." The "being-in-itself," unrelated to others or to itself, becomes consciousness in man. It questions itself and refers itself to the world. This is the "for-itself," a spark surrounded by the night. The "for-itself," or the presence to itself, produces "Nausea." For "there is nothing left in heaven, no Right or Wrong, nor anyone to give me orders," exclaims Orestes in *The Flies.* And then, as Simone de Beauvoir puts it, "whether there is anyone in the depths of heaven is no concern of man!"

In his little book *Existentialism and Humanism* Sartre declares that his philosophy is "a doctrine which does render life possible." "There is no sense in life *a priori.* Life is nothing until it is lived." It is the man who gives a meaning to life, for it is he who exists. And "he exists only in so far as he realizes himself; he is therefore nothing else but the sum of his action, nothing else but what his life is . . . Man makes himself . . . he makes himself by the choice of his morality." He defines himself, as far as he can be defined, by a "commitment." Sartre wants to help man. His existentialism is a humanism. It is "not atheist in the sense that it would exhaust itself in demonstrations of the non-existence of God. It declares, rather, that even if God existed that would make no difference. What man needs is to find himself again and to understand that nothing can save him from himself, not even a valid proof of the existence of God . . . It is only by self-deception, by confusing their own despair with ours that Christians can describe us as without hope." But he recognizes that "man is in anguish." This means that by committing himself he acknowledges his responsibility: he chooses not only his own being but all of humanity. Nonetheless, in contrast with classical humanism, man is not treated as his own end. "An existentialist will never take man as the end, since man is still to be determined." He does not shut himself up in himself, but remains "for ever present in a human universe." He projects himself beyond himself, and so causes himself to exist. His choice, which is inevitable and commits all mankind, is nothing to do with a free act, a caprice, as Gide would have it. Though it does not spring from any pre-established values, it will not be without merit. Man is sure of that. Does Sartre, then, provide a remedy, a solution for man's despair? He gives no proof of it. He is right, of course, when he says that the Christian, too, despairs of man. This is true in Pascal's sense, that man is all misery and weakness and must look to God for everything, for without him he can do nothing. What is man's life, asks the Bible, but sorrow and vanity? But Christianity transfigures this life from above. It believes that heaven has already visited the earth. For Sartre, on the other hand, there is no transfiguration, no justification, no beatitude. There is no salvation for man: he is "a useless passion." There is no more hope; nothing is left but to live one's life, even though the really human life "begins on the far side of despair."

Does Sartre believe that this far side exists? Although he is sometimes very near to Nietzsche, although he declares like Zarathustra that the "death of God" liberates man, he nowhere states that the liberty recovered by the disappearance or rather elimination of the Supreme Being enables man to transcend himself. Nietzsche, of course, exalted this transcending and, in spite of his almost satanic hatred of Christianity, necessary for the strong and the supermen, he offers his own Christ as a model. Not the "pale Galilean," necessary for the weak and the failures, still less the Saviour promising other-worldly rewards, but a strange character, constantly turned in on himself, on his inner world, in which he finds intense happiness and profound peace. To those who will follow him Nietzsche promises access to the only true kingdom of heaven within themselves. That is their one hope. Sartre does not appear to share it. If in places he seems a Nietzschean, he is nearer to Marxism, since it is men's destiny of which he thinks.

With the Marxists, he sees "no salvation for man" except in "the liberation of the working class." But he will have none of the materialist's faith, because he does not agree to renounce the rights of free criticism, evidence or truth. Sartre notes that "millions of men find in it [materialism] a hope and the image of their condition," and concludes that it enshrines some truths, but that does not mean that it is "entirely true as a doctrine." It is only a myth.

That, at least, was what the philosopher thought in 1946. It is possible that he has since developed, but all the same, he has scarcely convinced us that his existentialism is a humanism, this thinker for whom "hell is . . . other people!", who seems influenced by auto-eroticism, and concludes with the theory of nihilism.

Very different is Albert Camus, who has often been compared with him. He parted definitely and publicly with Sartre and they exchanged some sharp letters. Camus, moreover, cannot resign himself to the absurdness of life, and this is the ground of debate between him and Sartre. He sees only one question of importance for man: should he, or should he not, commit suicide? The logic of life implies suicide.

But actually he is the man in revolt. *L'Étranger* is the man who agrees to live, literally, as a stranger to himself, to his own destiny in the life beyond. He wagers for the present, against the future, against the Eternal, without hope. Sisyphus is content to toil up the cliff, his feet ever slipping on the scree. That is his personal, present destiny, which has nothing to do with some "higher destiny . . . This universe henceforth without a master seems to him neither sterile nor futile . . . The struggle itself towards the heights is enough to fill a man's heart. One must imagine Sisyphus happy." His happiness, precisely as a man, consists in doing something for one of his fellows, for the good of mankind. Thus the Algiers doctor, in *La Peste*, has no desire for holiness or a halo, the reward of the just in some other, higher world. The genuine *Justes* build their real, final city on earth. This cannot be the City of God and of grace. It is the city of revolt. By opting for this, man will be choosing solidarity, brotherhood, comradeship. "These are the true riches, for they are perishable," and Camus goes so far as to say: "The Christian society with its faith seems despairing." Not that he does not admire Christianity. But he still thinks that the created world is his only country, the flesh his only certainty, and that "understanding" dies with it.

In one of his Essays, called *Noces* (Marriage), he clarified his views about his world. This passage is worth quoting:

"I had spent my morning in a Franciscan monastery at Fiesole, full of the scent of the laurels. I had stopped a long time in a little court overflowing with red flowers, sunshine, black and yellow bees . . . Before going there I had visited the friars' cells and seen their little tables, each with a skull on it. And now the garden gave sign of their inspiration. I had gone back towards Florence, along the hill sloping down towards the town, open to view with all its cypresses. This splendour of the world, these women, these flowers, seemed to me the justification of those men. I wondered if they might also be the justification of all those men who realize that a certain extreme of poverty is always found along with the luxury and wealth of the world. Between the life of those Franciscans, shut away within their columns and their flowers, and that of those young folk on the Padovani beach at Algiers, who spend the whole year in the sun, I felt a mutual harmony. If they are stripped of everything, it is for the sake of a fuller life, not of another life. That, at least, is the only rightful use of the word *dénuement*. To be stripped always implies a sense of physical freedom and that accord between the hand and the flowers; that lover-like understanding between the earth and men sets one free from the human. If it were not already my religion, how gladly would I be converted to it! [And later:] The secret smile of Giotto's St. Francis justifies those who have the taste for happiness. [The Franciscans of Fiesole among their flowers had] Florence at their windows and death on their tables. A certain continuity in despair can give birth to joy."

In passing we must note this concept of a "joy of the sun," which is the wealth of the poor. Camus returns to it in other essays, originally published when he was twenty-two, which he ended by republishing, without quite recapturing the style of those pages. In the preface to *l'Envers et l'Endroit* he writes "Poverty has never been an evil to me: light flooded it with its riches. Even my rebellions were lit up with it. I think I can honestly say that they were always rebellions for all men, so that the life of all men might be lifted up to the light." After receiving the Nobel Prize for Literature the author, in his *Discours de Suede*, again returned to the ideas of his youth which he had never abandoned. Please God, this noble son of the Mediterranean, who believed in the splendour and "the beauty of the world", may have come to see before his death that they are but the reverse side of a splendour and a beauty whose name is God.

Earlier than Sartre and Camus, the philosopher and dramatist Gabriel Marcel had very soon come to know that life is both communion and mystery. Because it is communion, it establishes relations with the world. Because it is mystery, these relations do not derive from objectivity. They are not objects, presented to apprehension and understanding from without. Being is not reduced to having, and cannot become a problem. It is by meditation on his body that certain values are revealed to man. Thus in loving, another person is changed into a "thou" and a "presence" for the one who loves. The "I" finds a "thou". All the more does this prove true for the believer. In faith and recollection he discovers God, the "absolute Thou". He commits himself to the purely divine and is raised up to it. Now he can recognize God and bear witness to his ineffable, "transcendent" presence. But he must accept him and call upon him: his questioning must become invocation. If he is humble, he cannot refuse to pray. He will remain faithful and hold himself at the service of the things of God. He will foster the hope of being united to him, inasmuch as man, a traveller in this soulless world and bowed down under its technical sciences, is tempted to despair and suicide, and is in danger, too, of destroying the nobler values by regarding them as objects. But if he does, being is no more than having, presence is but matter, the person an image or a specimen, and God an idol. Man can only overcome these trials and conquer human anguish by coming to him "whose true name only religion knows": to God, his peace and his beatitude.

When They First Shot the Tall American

by Richard Gehman

The first day Gary Cooper spent as a cowboy extra is described in an amusing way in this passage taken from The Tall American: The Story of Gary Cooper.

As SOON AS HE [Cooper] arrived [at the studio], he found that all his diligent clothes-seasoning work of the previous afternoon had been for naught. Along with twenty-odd cowboys who had been hired for this sequence, he was issued a United States Cavalry uniform. The sleeves were too short and the breeches were too tight. "Never mind that," the unit director snapped. "You're not going to be in any close-ups, and the audience will never know the difference."

While the cameramen were getting their equipment in order, the director explained the scene. The Cavalry had been chasing a band of Indians for many miles, and now had them surrounded. "The first take will be a charge across the prairie, toward that tree over yonder. You'll start when I fire this gun. First man there gets an extra dollar—so go as fast as you can."

Cooper lined up with the rest of the troops. As far as he could see, he was the only man in a private's uniform. All the rest were wearing officer's insignia.

He patted his horse on the neck. It felt good to have a horse under him again, and he could hardly wait for the signal to gallop. It came before he was ready: *Crack!* went the director's gun, and the horsemen spurred their mounts into action. Cooper was taken by surprise. His horse reared and nearly threw him, but he held on, dug in his spurs, and soon caught up to the fleeing troops. They reined up at the tree in a cloud of dust, and from far away they heard the director cry "Cut!"

Why, Cooper thought as they rode back to the camera location, this acting business is a cinch. Nothing to it.

A half-hour later he changed his mind. This time the troops were ordered to gallop into a grove of oak trees. It was a thick cluster, and the director insisted that his men had to ride directly into it. Cooper looked at the trees and their low-hanging branches and was about to protest, but thought better of it.

Crack! went the director's gun, and the men started off.

Just as he reached the trees, Cooper yanked on the horse's reins hard to stop him, but he was too late. A branch caught him by the shoulder and threw him off, and he narrowly missed being trampled by the onrushing horses behind him. He lay there, his face cut, his shoulder aching unbearably. Off in the distance he heard the director call, "Cut!" All around him he heard moans and groans. Some men actually had suffered broken arms and ribs. Nearly everybody had been hurt in some way; there were bodies all over the ground, and only a few of the troopers had managed to stay on their mounts.

"That was great!" the director cried as he ran up. "Very

realistic, very true to life."

It was lunch time. Still feeling shaken, Cooper walked slowly to the commissary tent. He got his plate of pork and beans from the surly cook behind the serving table and went and sat down beside one of his fellow cowboy extras. The man nodded curtly and asked him where he was from. Cooper told him.

"First day?"

"Yup."

"You picked a bad one. It's not always this bad, but sometimes it's worse."

"What about those fellows who got hurt?" Cooper asked.

"Oh, they'll be back in action in a month or two. They always come back. Look at this." The man held out his right arm. It was as crooked as a forked branch. "Three breaks in that there. But you know, you can't beat the money. And it sure is better'n cow-punchin'."

They finished their beans and strolled out of the tent. The troopers—and some replacements for the injured—were beginning to assemble. Cooper felt someone pull at his sleeve. There was the director, a strange smile on his face. "You're Cooper?"

"That's right, sir."

"The casting department tells me they hear you're a good trick rider. Somebody said you're the best that ever came out of Montana. That true?"

Cooper hesitated. "Well . . . I wouldn't say it myself, but I've been told I can . . ."

"Good!" The director cut him off. "I need somebody to do a fall for me this afternoon. An easy fall from a horse— and he doesn't have to hit the ground with you. All you have to do is fall off. You can do that, can't you?"

"I reckon I can, sir."

"This is going to be *all your scene,*" the director said. "You'll be *the star* of it."

"That's mighty nice," Cooper said, but he did not trust the man's smile.

His apprehension increased when he saw the horse he was to ride. The mount of the morning had been a good, reliable range horse, spirited but obedient. This one was an earth-bound Pegasus. He was a stallion who did not like to be ridden, and he leaped and plunged when the budding actor finally got astride.

The scene called for Cooper to ride the horse at full gallop through a storm of arrows from the Indians. "Don't worry about it," the director called. "We've got expert archers here —they'll aim to miss you." Then he fired his blank pistol.

Cooper dug his heels into the horse, and they were off. Everything was going well, and he was in full control, until the arrows began whizzing by. The horse reared and bolted, and Cooper lost control. From far off, he heard the director shout, "Hit the dirt!" It was a welcome cry; if it had not come, he would have jumped from the maddened horse just to get away from him. In amateur rodeos in Montana, he had learned how to fall from a galloping horse and had become proficient. All a rider had to do was let his weight fall on an outstretched arm, push with that arm, and roll on his shoulder, over on his back. He dived, putting out his arm—but the horse was going so fast his arm bent in two. He hit the ground with his shoulder, and his momentum carried him up, over, and around a second time, a double somersault that landed him on his head.

He lay there wondering if this was what death was like. The doctor rushed up, bent and poked at him. "Aw, shucks," the doctor said to the director. "Shook up a little, that's all. He's fakin'."

If Frank Cooper, a peaceable young man, had had the strength, he would have pulled himself to his feet and punched the doctor's nose. There was only one consolation. After fifteen minutes, they still had not caught the horse.

The director sauntered by to where Cooper was sitting, knees drawn up, head between them, trying to get his breath, wishing the pains would go away.

"Not bad," he said. "Maybe we can use you again sometime, Cooper."

The director would have had the same gift that Cooper had ready for the doctor; but he backed away, hastily. Eventually, Cooper pulled himself to his feet. He went over to the pay tent.

"Because you did a spill, you get ten dollars," the teller said. "Otherwise you'd only get five—first day's work, and all."

"Thanks a lot," Cooper said. But his sarcasm was lost on the man.

Never again, he told himself. Easy money was not worth that kind of punishment. Also, he had resented the casual, scornful way the director and everybody else had treated the cowboy extras. My first and last day in pictures, he thought.

But on the way home, he began to feel a little better. The smog that now covers Los Angeles in layers was not there then, and the air was clean and fresh. A few breaths, and somehow the bruises did not bother him as much as they had after the two spills. The ten dollars crackled in his pockets. Somewhere inside him a voice said that he had been nervous because it had been his first day. He had ridden worse horses in Montana. He had just not warmed up properly to that horse; given another day, he could take the spill in his own stride, not the horse's. He grinned at his own foolishness. The next time he would size up his horse first and then take his spill. All he could think of was: ten whole dollars! And for falling off a horse!

In that moment all thoughts of making a success of his art work drained from his head. Later there were to be lingering doubts, but for now all he could think of was that he seemed, at last, to have found something he could do. He rushed home to tell his father, and they had the conversation with which this narrative opens. Judge Cooper finally gave his consent; his son could try acting for a year. And from that point on, Frank Cooper was a movie actor. . . .

Anglo-American Literature

An excellent example of literary criticism is this informative article from The Concise Encyclopedia of Modern World Literature *edited by Geoffrey Grigson.*

To ATTEMPT to survey, in a few paragraphs, the whole of twentieth-century literature in the English language—a literature which includes the poetry of South Africa, Australia and New Zealand, the intense novels about youthful alienation by Canadian novelists and the recent literary efflorescence in the West Indies, as well as the whole body of English and American literature—is to undertake an impossibility. Never have so many books been written and published, never have writers tried so hard to master their time in art. The novels of Joseph Conrad, D. H. Lawrence, E. M. Forster in England, and Henry James, William Faulkner and Ernest Hemingway in America; the poetry of T. S. Eliot and W. B. Yeats, Ezra Pound, W. H. Auden and Wallace Stevens—all this, to say nothing of many other major talents, represents a triumph for Anglo-American civilization and for the liberal ideal, a flowering of a dominant civilization.

Yet it is to some extent a hollow triumph, for there is increasing evidence that the artist's voice is a lonely one. Over this same period there has probably been less real interest in art in society at large, less conviction of its usefulness, than ever before. The separation of the serious artist from contact with a firmly felt audience, which had been won away, all but a few, by the less demanding non-artists of the mass-media, has gravely limited the artistic vision, and the artist has seen himself as more and more excluded from human councils. The influence exercised in the last century by novelists and poets has appeared to pass at the one extreme to the psychologists and sociologists, and at the other to film stars and singers; and in consequence the artist appears more than ever the marginal man, concerned with increasingly private problems presented in personal language and seemingly obscurantist techniques.

In short, the *avant-garde* revolution of the early years of the century, which was supposed to lead society into a finer world, simply separated the artist from his society; he led, but few followed. Movements such as the classicism of Eliot and others have had their relevance, but it seemed less and less to be a literary relevance. Though in both England and America the new century brought in many new names and new literary techniques, brought the experiments of James Joyce and Gertrude Stein, of Virginia Woolf and E. E. Cummings, brought the brilliant twenties with Aldous Huxley and Scott Fitzgerald, the socially conscious thirties with Auden and John Steinbeck, George Orwell, James Farrell, Erskine Caldwell and John Dos Passos, brought a steady expansion of the novel and of poetry and drama, the expansion came in steadily diminishing shocks. For one thing, war was so much more dramatic, so much more disintegrative of old ways of thinking and so much better at ushering in the new era of thought than ever art could be. Moreover, it may be that literature functions best when it is able to celebrate the dominion of man over his society; and the recurrent experience, and thus the recurrent artistic theme, of the twentieth century has been the capacity of society to triumph over man. It may be that literature is essentially a liberal endeavour, concerned with the freedom of man and with winning respect for his humanity, and that all modern literature has been able to show us is the failure of liberalism to protect itself against chaos. Surely what some of the differing works of our time, *Lady Chatterly's Lover* and *A Farewell to Arms*, *Dr. Zhivago* and *Sartoris*, *A Passage to India* and *The Waste Land*, have in common is the sense that it is hard enough for the respecter of individual virtue to protect even his own individuality in a world going rapidly away from the Golden Age. The artist, of course, sees as an artist, and has his own interest; and artists may be inclined to agree about the disastrous state of human affairs in a time when everyone is perfectly happy about his lot. But in a world in which the moral view of man has declined, the artist has been inclined to hold on to it; and Anglo-American literature has by and large defended liberalism and civilization at a time when they have been threatened from within and without. This is not an Anglo-American theme only; for one of the distinctive developments of the twentieth century has been the increasing internationalization of art. The writer writes for a world market; and he responds to the values of a world-wide audience.

The other great dilemma of the modern artist is that there is so much to know. There is (to use a phrase of André Malraux's) an "imaginary museum" of knowledge, traditional and international, which the artist has to master. It is harder than ever to play, so to speak, in the world league, to respond to the best that is known and thought in the world. It is difficult to find a style or a theme when all styles and themes seem to be exhausted, and when man himself is no longer impressed by grand designs. This is one reason why much modern art is concerned either with pursuing extreme originality, or with taking on the comic note and the wry theme, or with being unashamedly provincial. A novelist like Samuel Beckett seems to typify all three strains. And in English writing at least there has been an evident closing in of interests; we have had a Silver Age, since the last war, with poetry ever more personal and private and with the novel ever more restricted and provincial. The exceptions to the case—let us say, for instance, Lawrence Durrell in the novel, Dylan Thomas and the Beat Generation in poetry—have staked their attempts almost entirely in language and rhetoric, or have simply tried to live their art in their lives. England has its remarkable writers—Graham Greene and Ivy Compton-Burnett, C. P. Snow and William Golding and Iris Murdoch —but it cannot at present claim any younger writers of the first rank. When the gap is remarked on, which happens rarely, it is suggested that the impetus that used to be in the novel is now in the drama. But a close look there among the Osbornes and Weskers seems to show high competence but nothing more.

Can it be that we in England have grown provincial, that our interests generally are more limited than ever before and that we are either all too satisfied with things as they are or seeking only the rewards of social revolution, rewards which are, more conspicuously then ever, material? It would be a strange shift of balance if England now became the literary follower, and America the new cultural capital. For until the twenties America was very consciously the distant literary province, away from London, and so out of touch. London, one of the great cultural capitals, was a centre of English-language literature, drawing Oscar Wilde and Bernard Shaw, George Moore and Yeats, Joyce and J. M. Synge from Ireland, Eliot and Pound and James from America, Conrad from Poland. There was an international republic of letters, and to keep up, to be in the right place at the right time, was the essence of it.

The twenties and thirties were the period of great growth in American letters, bringing to notice novelists of the calibre of Hemingway, Fitzgerald, Faulkner, Nathaniel West, Dos Passos, and John O'Hara, and poets from Wallace Stevens to Robinson Jeffers. American literature was now distinctively itself; the new writers had an evident American stamp about them. Though many of their themes were international ones, and though they worked in conscious relation to the English literary tradition, it was to the American past that they looked most—to Whitman and Mark Twain, in particular, with their freedom of line, their vernacular style, their lack of interest in social themes and their preference for naked unsocial man, and with their large sense of responsibility for the quality of American society and the nature of American man. It is true that this stand often manifested itself in a desire to *épater le bourgeois*, to satirize the narrowness and provincialism of their country and to take the cynical view. But this was part of a wider alienation felt by American writers from American life, part of a sense that those who carried artistic and moral responsibility were quite cut off from those who carried political, economic and social responsibility. In one sense, the depression at the end of the twenties might be described as a consequence of the situation, and thereby its solution. For the Crash seemed to invite writers to take up once again their social duties— and the thirties were in America, as in England, the era of political literature, from *The Grapes of Wrath* by Steinbeck to *Waiting for Lefty* by Clifford Odets.

If writers can be said to embody some of the energy and curiosity of the society out of which they come, then in the end perhaps American writers were, and still are, more stimulated by their circumstances and nationality than they realized. American culture is a cosmopolitan, a borrowing culture, because America is a borrowing society. English letters today seem narrow and out of touch in comparison with the energy and eclecticism of American writing—writing that comprehends the violent decadence of Tennessee Williams and Truman Capote, the sophisticated mysticism of J. D. Salinger and John Updike, the protest of Negroes like Richard Wright, the turbulence of Norman Mailer, the bright Jewish affirmation of Saul Bellow and Bernard Malamud. Perhaps the balance is changing, perhaps the expatriation of English writers to America is a sign that the new capital of Anglo-American writing in the context of the international republic of letters is now no longer London but New York. But mutual influence remains, and one of the determinants of modern English letters is the apprehension of the English-American audience for which the modern author writes. The sense of common tradition—though within that tradition there are different paths and different solutions to common problems —has surely become stronger and the American performance is showing the English imagination ways of seeing that it might not have reached alone. It is less and less with the Continent, more and more with the States, that English writers are finding literary kinship.

Anglo-American civilization has played in the nineteenth and twentieth centuries a part comparable to that played by French civilization in the eighteenth century or Italian civilization at the Renaissance. The flowering of democratic liberalism that it represents is reflected in its literary production. Though it may be foolhardy to try to represent the nature and the variety of that production, it is worth insisting that it has taken advantage of the economic and political power of its two nations to address the world and to dramatize for it the fullness and folly of our values.

Mussolini's End

by Ivone Kirkpatrick

From Ivone Kirkpatrick's definitive biography, Mussolini: A Study in Power, *comes this dramatic passage which combines narrative skill and historical accuracy.*

THE COMBINED column moved out of Menaggio before dawn on April 27. With it traveled Elena Curti, Clara Petacci, and her brother Marcello. At about 7 A.M. they had reached Musso, where they were suddenly halted by a partisan roadblock. There was a brisk exchange of fire between the small partisan band and Pavolini's armored car, after which a white flag was hoisted and parleys began. It was about six in the morning. The local commander, Pier Luigi Bellini delle Stelle (Pedro), commanding the 52nd Garibaldi brigade, was summoned from his headquarters at Dongo a mile away to negotiate with the German officers. He explained that he was under instructions not to allow anyone to pass and the Germans retorted that they intended to carry out their orders to proceed to Merano. They added that they had no desire to enter into any conflict with the partisans. It seemed as if the parleys were deadlocked.

Both sides were, however, animated by the same purpose. Pedro's small, badly armed force was in no state to engage the Germans, whereas the Germans were only concerned to go home and had no stomach for a fight. The partisan tactics were to gain time and to rely on bluff. It was eventually agreed that the German commander, Lieutenant Fallmeyer, who had declared himself indifferent to the fate of the Italians attached to his convoy, should proceed with Pedro to partisan headquarters at Morbegno, some fifteen miles to the northeast, to discuss an accommodation.

The convoy waited at the lakeside for nearly six hours. Eventually at about two o'clock Fallmeyer returned with the news that the partisans, who were determined to prevent the passage of any Italians, had made preparations to blow a bridge on the river Mera, nine miles to the north. They were, however, prepared to permit the Germans to proceed on condition that they allowed their vehicles to be inspected at Dongo to ensure that they contained no Italians. Fallmeyer pressed this solution on Birzer, who felt that he had no alternative but to comply. His little escort would have been insufficient to protect the Duce in an area now completely in rebel hands.

As a last expedient Birzer induced Mussolini to don a German greatcoat and helmet and to enter one of the German trucks. He hoped that in this disguise the Duce might escape attention at the control post in Dongo. Mussolini, like a man in a dream, climbed obediently into the truck, taking with him his precious pouch of secret papers. At the last moment Clara attempted to join him, but she was stopped by the Germans and compelled to return to her brother's car at the rear of the column.

At about three o'clock the Germans moved off, leaving Mussolini's followers in the hands of the partisans. Mussolini was now completely alone. Within a few minutes the column halted in the square at Dongo, where the agreed inspection was to take place. Lieutenant Fallmeyer accompanied the partisans in their search of each vehicle, and eventually the huddled figure in the German uniform was recognized as the Duce. There is little doubt that his presence in the convoy had been reported by the partisans at Musso. He was immediately hauled out of the truck by his exultant captors and taken through an angry, excited crowd to the Municipality. According to Urbano Lazzaro (Bill), a second-in-command of the 52nd Garibaldi brigade, his face was waxen and his fixed, somewhat detached expression revealed an immense weariness, but not fear. He seemed to be bereft of will and spiritually dead. At last he was free from German tutelage. The German column, relieved of their incubus, gratefully pursued their march northwards.

Shortly afterwards Mussolini was joined in the municipal building by the remainder of his party, including Pavolini, who had been wounded in an attempt to escape by jumping into the lake. Marcello Petacci, who had attempted to pass himself off with a false diplomatic passport as a Spanish consul, had also been arrested with his family and Clara. He was detained in the local hotel for further investigation, while Clara, who had no papers and whose identity was still unsuspected, was consigned to the Municipality.

The capture of Mussolini, which was reported as soon as possible by telephone to Milan, was not an event with which the heterogeneous Committee of Liberation was equipped to deal. They were not a government, their members were scattered, and there was no machinery through which a quick decision could be reached in a matter of such importance. The immediate response was an instruction to treat the prisoner with every consideration and not to shoot, even if he should attempt to escape. It was evidently feared that the partisans might invoke the usual excuse for murdering a prisoner. But there was in Milan no clear idea as to what the next step should be. Only the Communists knew exactly what they wanted.

The Dongo partisans with fierce local pride seem to have been inspired by the desire to hold onto their important prize as long as possible, and in any event to surrender him to their superiors rather than to the Allies. Fearing that Mussolini might be snatched from them, they took him from the Municipality to the barracks of the Finance Guards at Germasino, in the mountains two miles from Dongo. There he was lodged in a cell, given supper, and, having regard to the instructions from Milan, invited to certify that he had been well treated. In a nervous hand he scribbled on a sheet of paper: "The 52nd Garibaldi Brigade captured me today Friday, April 27, on the square at Dongo. The treatment accorded to me during and after my capture has been correct." He seemed restless at times, his guards subsequently reported, but not afraid or in any way preoccupied with his fate.

He did, however, ask one favor of Pedro, the partisan commander: to say goodby on his behalf to Clara Petacci, who was under arrest in the Dongo Municipality, and to tell her not to think of him any more. This was the first intimation to the partisans that Clara was among the prisoners. Pedro duly carried out the commission and in a long interview with Clara, which he describes as affecting, eventually yielded to her entreaties to be allowed to rejoin her lover.

Meanwhile, later that night the partisans, fearing that

Mussolini's presence at Germasino had become generally known, decided to move him again, this time to a villa at San Maurizio near Brunate, two miles northeast of Como on the other side of the lake. He was awakened from his sleep, and, in order to disguise him as a wounded partisan on the way to the hospital, his head and face were so heavily bandaged as to render him unrecognizable. He submitted without a word to this treatment and was taken by car back to Dongo. It was raining heavily and very cold. On the square at Dongo Mussolini was allowed to alight to greet Clara Petacci. "Why have you decided to follow me?" Mussolini inquired, and she replied: "This is how I want it."

The party drove slowly in the direction of Como, Clara in a first car with a number of partisans and Mussolini in a second car, sitting behind with a woman partisan, who played the part of a nurse. On the way they were constantly stopped by partisan detachments at their road blocks, who allowed them to pass without much difficulty. When, however, they reached Moltrasio, four miles from Como, they heard the sound of distant firing, and they were told by a local friend that the Allies had arrived that night in Como, where they were meeting some residual resistance on the part of Fascist forces. Fearing that, if they persisted in trying to reach Brunate, they might become involved in the fighting or fall into the hands of the Allies or the Fascists, they decided to turn back to Azzano, ten miles away, close to which lived a small farmer known to one of them as a man who had harbored partisans. The cars stopped at the lakeside on the far side of Azzano and in the still pouring rain the weary party climbed the steep, rocky path to the village of Bonzanigo. The short journey took a quarter of an hour, and Clara in her high heels, supported on either side by Mussolini and Pedro, was so exhausted that she was obliged to stop for rest. Eventually they knocked at the farmer's door. It was now three o'clock on the morning of April 28. They were at once admitted, given coffee to drink, and lodged as well as circumstances permitted in a double-bedded room on the second floor. There they slept the sleep of exhaustion, while at Milan their fate was being debated.

So many contradictory accounts have been given of the proceedings of the Liberation Committee that it is impossible to determine exactly what occurred. It is, however, certain that the Communist members of the Committee were resolved to execute out of hand Mussolini and other members of the Fascist Republican government; and Togliatti subsequently claimed that he had given orders to this effect in his capacity of secretary of the Communist party and Vice-Premier of Italy. The members of the committee who made themselves responsible for carrying out Togliatti's order were Luigi Longo and Walter Audisio, a former volunteer in the Spanish Civil War, who went under the names of Giovanbattista di Cesare Magnoli and Colonel Valerio. It seems that these two men persuaded their colleagues of the committee to entrust Colonel Valerio with the mission of bringing Mussolini back to Milan, without revealing it was their intention that he should be brought back dead. In any event General Cadorna gave Valerio a pass, signed by the American liaison officer with the committee, requesting that he should be allowed to circulate freely in the execution of a mission entrusted to him by the National Liberation Committee.

Armed with this pass Valerio, accompanied by another trusted Communist, Aldo Lampredi, left Milan early on the morning of April 28 and drove to Como with an armed escort of partisans. At the prefecture he was received by the

new prefect, to whom he represented that he was under instructions to convey Mussolini and the other Fascists captured at Dongo to Milan. According to one of Valerio's many
subsequent accounts, the prefect displayed the petty jealou-
sies of a bourgeois spirit, or in other words showed reluc-
tance to allow Mussolini to be taken out of the hands of the
local partisans. There was a long, acrimonious discussion,
but Valerio's ruthless determination prevailed, and eventually he was allowed to pursue his way to Dongo.

There he arrived at about 2 P.M. only to find Pedro, the
local partisan commander, equally uncooperative. Valerio
was now in a frenzy. With every hour that passed the risk
increased that the Allies would intervene or that some other
circumstance would rob him of his prey. He brutally demanded that Pedro should forthwith hand over his prisoners,
and when Pedro demurred on the ground that the 52nd
Brigade, which had been responsible for their capture,
should deliver them to the Liberation Committee, he retorted: "There is no question of that. I have come to shoot
them." There was an altercation, but Valerio claimed that
he was acting under direct instructions from the Committee
and demanded a list of the Fascist prisoners at Dongo. When
this was produced, he announced that Mussolini and Clara
Petacci were to die. He then arbitrarily selected fifteen from
the list for execution, marking their names with a cross. Some
of the men were in the Municipality, while four had been
transferred during the previous night to the barracks at
Germasino. It was agreed that while Pedro drove to Germasino to bring back the four men to Dongo, Valerio should
proceed to Bonzanigo to fetch Mussolini and Clara. Pedro,
while submitting to superior orders, was still hoping that
the delay caused by this maneuver might yet frustrate Va-

lerio's design. Accordingly, Valerio departed on his errand, having discarded Pedro, and taking with him two reliable members of the local partisan brigade.

Mussolini had awakened late and, after a simple meal provided by the farmer's wife, had spent the day waiting. At about 4 P.M. on April 28 Valerio broke into his room and announced that he had come to rescue him. Mussolini and Clara Petacci were hurried down the stairs and along a narrow lane to a waiting car. They drove for about a mile down a narrow mountain road in the direction of the lake. Suddenly the car stopped outside the Villa Belmonte, a substantial house standing behind a low stone wall. Mussolini and Clara were ordered out of the car, quickly placed against the wall on the left side of the gate, and riddled with machine-gun bullets at almost point-blank range.

Two men were left to guard the bodies while Valerio returned immediately to Dongo to complete his bloody work. The fifteen men selected for execution were hurriedly brought out on the square and lined up facing the lake. The protests of the mayor were angrily brushed aside. Only three minutes were allowed for the ministrations of a priest and the prisoners were shot down by a partisan squad. Immediately afterwards Marcello Petacci was also executed.

The selections in Part Three: A Hawthorn Sampler have, no doubt, whetted your appetite for one or more of the books from which they were taken. These books are all on Hawthorn's current list and may be ordered from:

Hawthorn Books, Inc.
70 Fifth Avenue
New York, New York 10011

If you would like to go deeper into the subject of better reading for yourself, or your company, or your school, you may write directly to:

The Reading Laboratory, Inc.
370 Lexington Avenue
New York, New York 10017

THE AUTHOR AND HIS BOOK

WILLIAM S. SCHAILL was born in New York City in 1918 and now lives in Bronxville, New York. He was educated in the United States, France and England, and has traveled widely in Europe, South America and the Caribbean area. At one time he was a plantation owner in Virginia, along the James River. Later, he spent some time as a shark fisherman and as captain of a trading schooner. During World War II he served in the U. S. Navy and U. S. Coast Guard. A member of the Explorers Club and Dutch Treat Club, he has always been fond of the sea and sailing. In 1949, Mr. Schaill founded The Reading Laboratory, Inc., of New York City. In addition to this book, he has written and edited a great many articles and specialized materials in the field of developmental reading.

SEVEN DAYS TO FASTER READING (Hawthorn, 1965), was set in Bodoni Book, a type designed by Giambattista Bodoni in 1788 and a favorite of modern type users. The display type is Bauer Bodoni Extrabold Italic, which, unlike many other innovations on a designer's original concept, comes very near to being a faithful copy of the Italian designer's type. The book was printed and bound by Halliday Book Press, New York.

A HAWTHORN BOOK